AUTONOMY AND SYMPATHY

A Post-Kantian Moral Image

Filimon Peonidis

University Press of America,® Inc.
Lanham · Boulder · New York · Toronto · Oxford

Copyright © 2005 by
University Press of America,® Inc.
4501 Forbes Boulevard
Suite 200
Lanham, Maryland 20706
UPA Acquisitions Department (301) 459-3366

PO Box 317
Oxford
OX2 9RU, UK

All rights reserved
Printed in the United States of America
British Library Cataloging in Publication Information Available

Library of Congress Control Number: 2004116237
ISBN 978-0-7618-3080-1

⊖™ The paper used in this publication meets the minimum
requirements of American National Standard for Information
Sciences—Permanence of Paper for Printed Library Materials,
ANSI Z39.48—1984

KANT DO IT

Handwritten inscription on a copy of Kant's
Critique of pure reason
Borchardt Library, La Trobe Univesity

For Martha and Alexandros
my inner circle

Table of contents

Preface vii
Abbreviations xi
Acknowledgments xiii

1. Basic themes from Kant's ethics

1.1.	Preliminary remarks	1
1.2.	The *Groundwork of the metaphysics of morals*	3
1.2.1.	First part	3
1.2.2.	Second part	5
1.2.2.1.	The a priori basis of ethics (IV: 406-12)	5
1.2.2.2.	The notion of the categorical imperative. A reconstruction of Kant's syllogistic (IV: 412-20)	5
1.2.2.3.	The three formulations of categorical imperative and their relations (IV: 421-45)	7
1.2.3.	Third part. How are categorical imperatives possible or what is the ultimate condition of Kant's ethics?	13
1.3.	Morality, happiness and God	17
1.4.	*The metaphysics of morals* as a sequence to the *Groundwork*	19

2. Towards a post-Kantian moral image

2.1.	Maintaining distances from Kant	27
2.2.	The post-Kantian moral subject	32

3. Sympathy as a moral emotion

3.1.	Kant again	43
3.2.	The nature and value of sympathy	47
3.3.	Empirical findings	51

4. Autonomic obligations

4.1.	The image continued and completed	59
4.2.	Possible objections	65
4.3.	Epilogue	69

Bibliography 75
Index 81
About the author 85

Preface

This essay aims to combine three different general ideas. The first is that Kant's moral philosophy can be the starting point of a normative account that constitutes a live and plausible option for us. Of course, this does not imply a wholesale acceptance of everything the philosopher said, as it is up to us to decide which of his ideas continue to appeal to a modern audience after two centuries of innovative ethical theorizing and to incorporate them, even in modified forms, into a workable and coherent moral framework. This leads to the second idea, namely that it is necessary to combine Kantian and non-Kantian views alike, including those that assign a major role to emotions in understanding and justifying morality. The third idea is that we should keep in mind—to use Hume's phrase—that "the end of all moral speculations is to teach us our duty" or at least to provide us with some orientation in that messy field. And I take "us" to refer here to everyone concerned with moral issues and not to a handful of experts in academia. The last idea that cuts across the notion of "moral image" discussed in the book once sounded trivial, but it has to be re-emphasized after a century of intense metaethical discussion.

Along these lines I argue that individuals who value personal autonomy and feel sympathy for other human beings can be guided in their life by a set of general other-regarding obligations that reflect central values of the Western moral tradition. These obligations may not be able to help them decide what to do in every imaginable case, but their informed determination to act upon them is necessary for combating many serious and easily identifiable moral evils that beset us. The overall argument is called a *post-Kantian moral image*.

The essay's point of departure is a short overview of certain basic themes from Kant's ethics. I discuss the formulations of the categorical imperative in the *Groundwork of the metaphysics of morals*, the way Kant answers the question "how are categorical imperatives possible?" in the *Groundwork* and in the *Critique of practical reason*, the interplay between morality, happiness and God, and the more practical approach he adopts in *The metaphysics of morals*. Here I approach Kant's work in a rather charitable spirit and try to highlight the unity of his moral project and to defend it against certain common criticisms I find ill-founded (i.e. his alleged formalism). The purpose of this chapter is to usher in the subsequent argument and to acquaint the reader with the basic elements of Kantian ethics.

The exposition of the main argument starts in the second chapter. The tone changes as I begin with the discussion of four major objections to Kant's ethics which any modern normative discourse that draws heavily on it has to take into account. In particular, I argue that his refusal to allow exceptions to perfect duties, the restrictive identification of autonomy with obeying the moral law, the metaphysical idea of abstract rational beings that legislate devoid of all individual differences in a kingdom of ends, and his claim that reason itself can be the source and the motive for moral action can hardly convince the modern reader.

Next I proceed to sketch a post-Kantian moral image. A moral image is not a full-blown ethical theory that seeks to determine action to the last detail. It is rather a general and comprehensive pattern of moral argumentation that can serve as a guide to our moral considerations. It gives moral reflection momentum and a certain direction but lets the agent do the rest and decide where this direction leads in practice. The term "post-Kantian" means that the proposed moral image adopts certain elements from Kant's moral philosophy but goes beyond it in that (a) it rejects the aforementioned problematic parts of Kant's moral theory and (b) it incorporates an outlook that has been explicitly ruled out by Kant.

The moral image is deployed in three steps. In step one I imagine an ordinary individual (the post-Kantian moral subject) who seeks a moral framework for her life. The only condition she sets in advance is that her inquiry be devoid of any religious or metaphysical elements. The post-Kantian moral subject realizes that autonomy is a fundamental source of intrinsic and instrumental value in her life. Here autonomy means *feasible* autonomy and it is conceived as a constant effort to retain, *as far as possible*, the proper epistemic relation to the environment surrounding us, to avoid being carried away by urges and desires we do not approve of, and to act upon reflection. She also discovers that the same holds for other people, but this very finding does not motivate her to respect their autonomy.

In step two (chapter three) I assume that the post-Kantian moral subject can feel genuine *sympathetic concern* for other people. Sympathy is understood as a primitive emotion that is part of our psychological make-up. We experience this emotion when we see other people in distress or suffering, feel badly because of their plight, and are disposed to act, having their well-being as our ultimate goal. It is argued that sympathy has a prima facie moral value, since it implies benevolent action, and that it prepares the ground for acting on moral principles.

In step three (chapter four), having now assumed the sympathetic nature of the post-Kantian subject, I regard her as motivated to show respect for the autonomy of her fellow human beings, including those she will never know and never meet. Her respect is expressed in the form of a set of general obligations she acknowledges to owe to every human being, irrespective of any special relation, attachment or agreement. They include reverence for human life, truthfulness, the avoidance of force and coercion, tolerance, fair treatment as well as specific obligations of non-maleficence and assistance.

The moral image ends here. It cannot deal with the complications that arise as the subject moves to a further level of specification. These are not due so much to her motivational defects as to the peculiarity and the complexity of the moral situations she encounters. This is the price one pays as one descends from Kant's orderly heaven to the messy reality of human action and interaction, but it is a price worth paying. The account concludes with the discussion of two plausible objections that can be raised against the suggested moral image.

August 2004 F. P.
Kalamaria, Greece

Abbreviations

All references to the texts of Immanuel Kant are to their abbreviated title, their volume and page number in the Prussian Academy edition (Vols. I-XXIX, Berlin, 1902-) and the page number of their English translation (for example C, V: 7, 142). I use the following abbreviations and English translations:

A= *Anthropology from a pragmatic point of view* [1798]. Translated with an introduction and notes by Mary J. Gregor. The Hague: Martinus Nijhoff, 1974.
C= *Critique of practical reason* [1788]. In *Practical philosophy*. Translated and edited by Mary J. Gregor. General introduction by Allen Wood. Cambridge: Cambridge University Press, 1996.
CJ= *The critique of judgement* [1790]. Translated with analytical indexes by James Creed Meredith. Oxford: Clarendon Press, 1978.
CPR= *Critique of pure reason* [1781/1787]. Translated and edited by Paul Guyer and Allen W. Wood. Cambridge: Cambridge University Press, 1998.
G= *Groundwork of the metaphysics of morals* [1785]. In *Practical philosophy*. Translated and edited by Mary J. Gregor. General introduction by Allen Wood. Cambridge: Cambridge University Press, 1996.
I= "Idea for a universal history with a cosmopolitan purpose" [1784]. In *Kant's political writings*. Edited with an introduction and notes by Hans Reiss. Translated by H. B. Nisbet. Cambridge: Cambridge University Press, 1977.
L= "On a supposed right to lie from philanthropy" [1797]. In *Practical philosophy*. Translated and edited by Mary J. Gregor. General introduction by Allen Wood. Cambridge: Cambridge University Press, 1996.
LE= *Lectures on ethics*. Edited by Peter Heath and J. B. Schneewind. Translated by Peter Heath. Cambridge: Cambridge University Press, 1997.

Abbreviations

MM= *The metaphysics of morals* [1797]. In *Practical philosophy*. Translated and edited by Mary J. Gregor. General introduction by Allen Wood. Cambridge: Cambridge University Press 1996.

P= *Prolegomena to any future metaphysics that will be able to come forward as a science* [1783]. In *Theoretical philosophy after 1781*. Edited by Henry Allison and Peter Heath. Translated by Gary Hatfield, Michael Friedman, Henry Allison and Peter Heath. Cambridge: Cambridge University Press, 2002.

R= *Religion within the boundaries of mere reason* [1793]. In *Religion and rational theology*. Translated and edited by Allen W. Wood and George Di Giovanni. Cambridge: Cambridge University Press, 1996.

Acknowledgments

This essay originates from the research I did for a class on Kant's ethics I taught at the Aristotle University of Thessaloniki, a Greek draft of which was completed in September 2003 during a visit to La Trobe University. An earlier version of the core idea will appear in the *Journal of Philosophical Research* (Peonidis 2005) and I would like to thank its editor, Hugh McCann, for allowing me to reproduce material from this article. The quotations from the comprehensive volume Immanuel Kant *Practical philosophy* are reprinted with the kind permission of Cambridge University Press. At various stages of writing this essay I benefited from the comments, suggestions and criticisms of Laurence Thomas, Rüdiger Bittner, Stelios Virvidakis and Stathis Psillos as well as of audiences in Brussels, Melbourne and Athens. Special thanks are due to Ross Phillips and Anastasios Tamis of La Trobe University for the exceptional hospitality they offered me. Finally, I am grateful to Kathleen Hart for her painstaking assistance in preparing the final manuscript.

Chapter one

Basic themes from Kant's ethics

1.1. Preliminary remarks

Presenting even a concise and introductory account of the magisterial moral doctrine of Immanuel Kant (1724-1804) is no easy task. This is partly due to his declared conviction that the nature of the problems he discussed did not allow a simpler or more familiar language (C, V: 10, 145). Apart from this, one has to deal with layers of preconceptions and misconceptions concerning crucial points of his thought that have accrued after many years of (often superficial) criticism.[1] It is not far from the truth to say that with Kant, more than any other philosopher of the same stature, even the simplest attempt to describe his views is already an interpretation. Nevertheless, we do want a deeper understanding of his moral philosophy. Kant's work does not simply constitute one of the most original and groundbreaking contributions to the history of moral thought, but it contains principles, ideas and arguments one cannot afford to ignore.[2] The notions of respect for every human being and of the universalizability of maxims, the idea that the agent herself should be the sole source of any genuine moral conduct, and even the requirement to disregard altogether the consequences of an action when we are determining its moral worth, are all part of our moral framework. This does not mean, to be sure, that all the above positions are endorsed or realized by everyone. It means that they are associated with aspects of the current conception of the normative. In this sense our engagement with Kant's thought, as with Aristotle's and Mill's, is an *exercise in moral self-reflection.* Whether or not we accept what will ensue from it is a different question.

Kant's practical philosophy can be seen as an answer to the question "What should I do?" and to a lesser extent to the question "What may I hope for?". It is a bold answer that constitutes the articulation of a self-contained, complex moral theory, full of subtle distinctions and founded on the pure practical reason of autonomous beings. At the same time, it is an answer addressed to various philosophical opponents: those who, enchanted by the spectacular advances of the natural sciences, entertained serious doubts as to whether something analogous could ever be achieved in ethics; those who maintained that people were motivated only by self-interest; and those who, although they did not dispute the overriding character of morality, appealed to principles that for Kant were bogus or inappropriate such as happiness, the divine commands, perfection or an empirically defined moral sense. Kant himself did not believe that it would be easy for people to live by his own moral doctrine, since he did not underestimate the influence of non-rational forces on ordinary reasoning. His saying "nothing straight can be constructed from such warped wood as that of which man is made" (I, VIII: 23, 46) reflects his own pessimism.[3] Nevertheless, faithful to the general spirit of the Enlightenment, he was convinced that everyone was capable of moral progress. At any rate, he held that even if no one abided by the moral law, it would retain its unconditional value. The significance of moral principles lies in their nature, not in their popularity.

There is no doubt that Kant's most well-known and accessible moral treatise is the *Groundwork of the metaphysics of morals* (1785) (hereafter *Groundwork*). In this chapter I will follow in some detail the argument developed in this book, adding material from his other major ethical—or better metaethical—work the *Critique of practical reason* (1788) (hereafter second *Critique*). In addition, I will refer to the sequel to the *Groundwork*, *The metaphysics of morals* (1797), in which the philosopher sought to specify the more practical aspects of his doctrine.[4] It should be noted that there is also a *political* and *social* dimension to Kant's normative thought which has become a constant source of inspiration for many political and legal theorists during the last decades. His conception of a state in which the only permissible liberties for each of its members would be those compatible with the liberties of the rest, his notion of a hypothetical social contract, a rather "communitarian" conception of ownership, as well as his views on the preconditions for lasting peace among nations figure one way or another in many current discussions and debates that exceed the limits of Kantian scholarship, narrowly defined. However, here I shall confine myself strictly to his moral views.[5]

1.2. The *Groundwork of the metaphysics of morals*

Kant's main objective in this treatise is to seek the supreme principle of morals. A principle of this kind must express an internal necessity and be binding for all rational beings. Therefore, it cannot be sought in the always-changing world of experience or in the unstable and unruly realm of human psychology, but in the a priori concepts of pure practical reason. What is required is a *metaphysics* of morals, not a physics of morals or a *practical anthropology*, that is an empirical investigation of human moral behavior.[6]

Kant informs his readers that he intends to use the following method (G, IV: 392, 47-48): he will start from certain common and widely held conceptions and through an analysis of them arrive at the supreme principle of morals. Next he will return to ordinary moral thinking and reconstruct it grounded on the knowledge gained in the previous step. Yet in what follows Kant appears to be preoccupied with the first part of his method. The second part of it is more easily recognized in *The metaphysics of morals*.

1.2.1. First part

In the first part of the *Groundwork* Kant presents certain key terms of his moral philosophy and maintains that all these are part of everyone's innate moral make-up, albeit in a vague and rudimentary manner.[7] Next he sets out to define all these terms and to organise them into a coherent whole that could serve as the ultimate practical guide, by providing us reasons and motives for doing our duty and for overcoming the natural forces working against this. An exposition of the main points of the argument articulated in the first part of the treatise goes as follows:

a. If there is something unconditionally good, this is a *good will*.
b. Its value does not depend on the results it brings about but on what it desires and tries to achieve using all available means. Here Kant

wants to exclude the influence of various factors that are external to the will and that thwart its absolutely good intentions. The good will must be immune to (bad) moral luck. It retains its value intact even if it is prevented by uncontrollable circumstances from acting.[8]

c. The good will is subject to the influence and direction of reason.

d. Neither the good will nor reason has the pursuit of happiness as its proper function. This is accomplished by the instincts. Thus, reason's inability to secure happiness should not become a source of disappointment.

e. Reason seeks to create an inherently good will and this particular activity satisfies it.

f. The good will, which exists in everyone in a crude form, should be elucidated through an elaboration of the notion of *duty* that includes it.

g. If an action is contrary to duty or is simply done in conformity with it, it cannot be regarded as moral. Only actions done *from* duty (*aus Pflicht*) have moral worth. Here Kant does not express a strange "duty fetishism", as some may have thought, but merely claims that if we are to act morally in the proper sense, our sole reason and motive should be that we are doing the right thing as prescribed by an objective higher principle or law. In the second *Critique*, he will describe duty "as an action that is objectively practical in accordance with this law [the moral law] with the exclusion of every determining ground of inclination..." (C, V: 80, 205). Our dispositions, and even more our considerations of self-interest, have no place in the process of moral justification. The fact that I find pleasure in helping people in distress or that I believe that this will make me popular in my peer-group is irrelevant as a ground of genuine beneficent action. However, as it will be noted later, Kant admits that certain moral emotions may facilitate proper moral conduct, but he allows them no more than this auxiliary function.

h. The moral worth of an action done from duty does not lie in the goal it seeks to achieve but in the maxim to which it conforms. A maxim broadly conceived is a subjective principle of the will.

i. The maxim in accordance with which an action done from duty is decided should reflect "a sense of *respect for the universal moral law*". This sense exists in every rational being and thus the only guiding principle of the will is that "I ought never to act except in such a way that I could also will that my maxim should become a universal law" (G, IV: 402, 57). Nevertheless, although ordinary people show reverence for this principle, their ignorance of its origin and justification renders them vulnerable to all sorts of pressure to dismiss it in behalf of the pursuit of happiness or self-interest. Hence, the only way for ordinary human beings to escape from this uncomfortable position is to appeal to philosophy, which alone can offer them not only an objective account of their situation but of the means necessary to overcome it.

1.2.2. Second part
1.2.2.1. The a priori basis of ethics (IV: 406-12)

Kant devotes the first paragraphs of the second part of the *Groundwork* to explaining to his readers that it is futile to seek the ground of morality through inductive generalizations of observable human conduct. People do not appear to follow a consistent pattern of moral decision-making, let alone to be bound by duty. Moreover, on many occasions they give priority to their own interests, desires and urges, thus making the case for those who profess immoralism and egoism stronger. This is, however, no reason for embarrassment, since we are looking in the wrong place. Even if no one ever performed a moral act worthy of the name, reason would never cease to command us to do the right thing. Thus, if we are searching for the origin of the supreme principle of morality and if we want to determine what makes acting from it possible, we have to turn our attention to the a priori axioms of pure practical reason. Empirical examples are unhelpful at this stage, since they derive their own worth from presupposed rules and principles. What is needed is to leave behind the unstable and uncertain world of experience and become engaged in a metaphysical moral inquiry. This will necessarily lead us to a complicated investigation of rational nature in itself in its most abstract and pure form. From now on this will be Kant's major concern.

1.2.2.2. The notion of the categorical imperative. A reconstruction of Kant's syllogistic (IV: 412-20)

After this general statement of purpose, Kant presents a chain of arguments and assumptions that lead to a preliminary description of his key notion of the *categorical imperative*. His reasoning can be briefly reconstructed as follows:

a. Humans as rational beings have the will to act in accordance with the representation of objective practical laws.

b. If reason could determine our will absolutely and without any external interference, then our actions would be subjectively and objectively necessary. In this case we would have a holy (*heilige*) will for which it would be natural to conform to the law. Such a will would find the notion of "ought" meaningless.[9]

c. If, however, the determination of our will by reason is not absolute, if, in other words, our will is influenced by our instincts, interests or inclinations, then our actions are objectively necessary but subjectively contingent.

d. In this case reason forces itself upon the will, since its obedience is uncertain.

e. The representation of objective and unrestricted practical law, insofar as it necessitates the will, is called a command of reason and is expressed in the form of an imperative (you ought to x). It should be noted that this is an internal necessitation and has nothing to do with the external necessitation that is commonly associated with penalties or rewards (as is the case in law).

f. Imperatives are classified into *hypothetical* (*hypothetisch*) and *categorical* (*kategorisch*). The hypothetical ones specify the means necessary for achieving a particular purpose; they instruct us how to fulfil our ends but they never pass judgment on these very ends. They are expressed in the form "if you want y, then you ought to do x". On the contrary, categorical imperatives, which as representations of the moral law are the imperatives of morality, command certain actions to be performed because of their nature and origin and not because of their consequences or because they would bring about a desired end. Their categorical character means that they prescribe actions that are necessary and unconditional (you ought to do x—period!).

g. Hypothetical imperatives in their turn are divided into *technical* and *pragmatic*. The former concern skills and are related to subjective ends ("if you want to become really good at chess, you have to practice everyday"). The latter have a prudential character in the sense that they tell people how to promote their own welfare ("if you can't stand the heat, stay out of the kitchen"). Their prescriptions are more universally binding compared to the technical ones, but their universality is limited by the fact that people differ significantly in their conceptions of welfare.

h. Imperatives in general are distinguished from maxims, which, as previously mentioned, are merely subjective principles of the will.

i. Kant ends this section by wondering how imperatives are possible. This calls for an inquiry into the procedures through which we conceive imperatives as necessary and incumbent upon our will. When we have to deal with hypothetical imperatives, the answer is relatively easy, since it is analytically true that if we want our aims to be fulfilled, then we must necessarily want any means that can realize them. Regarding pragmatic imperatives, in particular, our choice of means is often unfortunate so they should be better viewed "as counsels (*consilia*) rather than as commands (*praecepta*) of reason" (G, IV: 418, 71).

j. However, when it comes to the possibility of categorical imperatives, nothing is self-evident. The imperatives of morality are a priori *synthetic* propositions meaning in a Kantian context (a) that the predicate concept is not contained in the subject concept and (b) that they are not given by experience. In fact they tell us something about the sensible world—they instruct us about what we have to do here and now—but they do not originate in this world. Thus their possibility cannot be secured by an inquiry into their meanings or by referring to certain examples of (supposed) actual compliance with them. These examples may be widely off the mark and have no explanatory force.

At this point Kant states that the resolution of this crucial issue can be postponed until we have a better understanding of the content of the categorical imperative. The question will be taken up again in the third part of the *Groundwork*.

1.2.2.3. The three formulations of the categorical imperative and their relations (IV: 421-45)

If a categorical imperative is a representation of a command issued by the unrestricted moral law, then there is only one categorical imperative:

> Act only in accordance with the maxim through which you can at the same time will (*kannst wollen*) that it become a universal law (G, IV: 421, 73).

Kant also gives another slightly different formulation in which the term universal law is replaced by the term "universal law of nature"[10] and then he discusses four specific maxims that fail to satisfy the requirements of the categorical imperative and are thus to be rejected as principles of moral action. The conclusion drawn from this discussion is that a rational being is not allowed to (a) commit suicide out of self-love in order to avoid a life full of misery, (b) give promises she does not intent to keep, (c) leave her talents undeveloped and (d) remain indifferent to the misfortunes of her fellow humans.

The interpretation of the first formulation and the examples that are supposed to shed light on it is one of the most controversial issues in Kantian scholarship.[11] Given the introductory and concise character of this account, I will put forward only my own understanding of it, supported, as far as possible, by the necessary textual evidence. A good starting point would be to ask why Kant chooses to use the formula "you can...will that it become a universal law" instead of simply saying "you will that it become a universal law". One reasonable explanation is that he wants to avoid the possibility of certain maxims that are generally recognized as irrational or morally reprehensible to pass the test of the categorical imperative. For instance, someone would like to give the status of universal law to her maxim that gratuitous self-mutilation (i.e. with no survival value) is an act of absolute self-control and someone else could have the same thoughts concerning her subjective principle that the powerful should dominate the weak, even if she counts herself among the weak (or she realises that someday she is likely to become one of them). If the categorical imperative allowed such maxims to become universal laws, that is laws binding for everyone, then the charge that Kant's formalism is unable to draw the line between right and wrong principles of action would not be unfounded.

We can have a better grasp of the issue if we ask what maxims I *cannot* will to become a universal law. There seems to be two sorts of them: those which, when universalized, would be *self-defeating*, and those that *conflict with human rational nature*.

Consider the following passage:

> Some actions are so constituted that their maxim cannot even be *thought* without contradiction as a universal law of nature, far less could one *will* that it *should* become such. In the case of others that inner impossibility is indeed not to be found, but it is still impossible to *will* that their maxim be raised to the universality of a law of nature because such a will would contradict itself (G, IV: 424, 75).

The first type of maxim does not raise many doubts; if "ought implies can", one should not act on maxims that cannot possibly become universal laws. The maxim "I should make promises I do not intend to keep" clearly belongs to this category, since if everyone started acting on this, and (given the public character of universal law) this became common knowledge, there would then be mutual distrust and the very notion of promise would become obsolete. In this sense I cannot even think of it as a universal law. However, if I focus on the remaining examples of unacceptable maxims, I can think of situations where people would put an end to their lives in dire circumstances, they would spoil their natural talents or they would not help anyone in distress. Perhaps the world would not be such a good place to live, but no "inner contradiction" arises. Then, why should I not will these three maxims to become a universal law? It is reasonable to assume that for Kant the will contradicts itself in all these cases. This is a rather vague position but it can be construed in the following way: the will of a rational human being contradicts itself if it acts in an *irrational* manner. In his words a rational being cannot disregard her talents, since they are useful to her in various ways, nor can she behave callously thus depriving her of the opportunity of receiving any assistance in the future. As for suicide, it seems irrational to desire to shorten our lives out of self-love, when this same emotion always urges us to carry on living (G, IV: 422-23, 74-75).[12]

If Kant's discussion of the categorical imperative were to come to an end at this point, his conception of rational human nature would imply nothing more than being consistent and acting according to one's best interests. This is what we infer from the reasons he offers against the three aforementioned maxims. If this were the case, his overall project would be doomed to failure, as the most he could achieve would be to found morality on a posteriori self-interest. This is why he makes his next major move to upgrade rational nature from something prudentially valuable to the supreme principle of a morality that is not limited to human beings. Rational nature in general devoid of all its empirical elements now becomes an end in itself.

> If, then, there is to be a supreme practical principle and, with respect to the human will, a categorical imperative, it must be one such that, from the representation of what is necessary an end for everyone because it is an *end in itself*, it constitutes an *objective* principle of the will and thus can serve as a universal practical law. The ground of this principle is: *rational nature exists as an end in itself* (G, IV: 428, 79).

Therefore, if we are to acknowledge and respect rational nature as such (both in ourselves and in others), we should never use any human being as a means to some end. Not doing this means that we admit that rational nature is subordinate to some higher principle. Thus, we arrive at the second formulation of the categorical imperative:

> So act that you use humanity, whether in your own person or in the person of any other, always at the same time as an end, never merely as a means (*bloß als Mittel*) (G, IV: 429, 80).

Thus, an agent who wants her maxims to become universal law does not adopt maxims that either are self-defeating or constitute an affront to rational nature in the sense of treating others (or herself) merely as means. Kant uses exactly the same examples to show that the aforementioned maxims are incompatible with the second formulation of the categorical imperative.

Why does Kant say "only as means"? It is a truism that in everyday life we take advantage of the expertises and positions of an indefinite number of people to achieve simple or complex personal aims. For instance, we use the bus driver to get to our destination and the bank teller to cash a check. In a sense we treat all these persons as means. However, there is nothing morally wrong with this provided that we show respect for the persons with whom we communicate and interact. On the contrary, if we just want to impose our will upon them by violating all the rules and conventions governing our relations with them (as in a bus high-jacking or a bank robbery) or we are even willing to harm them to carry out our plans, then it is obvious that we treat them *only* as means and not as ends in themselves. This way of understanding the locution "only as means" makes Kant's position plausible.

Perhaps one can find the second formulation quite vague for it does not specify at least the *types* of actions it prohibits. The four examples discussed in the text provide little guidance to the reader. This worry can be envisaged as associated to the general criticism that Kant is interested only in the form of moral judgments and not in their content. Yet it would be a mistake to assume that we are dealing with a formal principle here. Kant demands that we honor rational nature as such and the best way to do this is to treat rational beings as ends in themselves. As to his reluctance to move to a higher level of specificity, it is up to us to fill in the gap left by Kant.

Hence we can distinguish certain types of actions that are ruled out by the second formulation. These include:

a. The direct infliction of bodily or mental harm upon others or the threat of inflicting it to further personal ends.

b. Lying and deception. Deceitful persons attempt to appropriate and manipulate the cognitive processes of other people to impose false beliefs on them. Thus, at first sight they use them only as means.

c. Exploitation. Persons practicing exploitation are engaged in relations from which they seek to receive as many benefits as possible at the least cost to themselves. This betrays a blatant disrespect for their fellow humans.[13]

d. Hard paternalism. This term is used to describe the intervention in a competent adult's life, in ways she does not consent to, for beneficent reasons. Here the person who intervenes does not use others as a means to promote her own personal ends but to advance the interests she believes other people *should* have, even if these people think differently.[14] Again this is a form of disrespect (although a subtler version) of rational nature.

Of course, I am not saying that these are the only types of action rendered inappropriate by the second formulation or that all these prohibitions are absolute. Moreover, I am not claiming that Kant would approve this particular interpretation of his principle, although it can be inferred from the available evidence that he would condemn most of these types of action. My point is simply that the second formulation provides us with a general moral framework that enables us to come up with substantive principles that are faithful to the spirit—but not necessarily to the letter—of Kant's thought.

Nevertheless, Kant believes that something is missing from his account. In particular, someone could follow the prescriptions of the categorical imperative passively and perfunctorily, without having a clear view of exactly what she is doing, simply because this has been inculcated in her by society or religion. Such an agent does not exhibit a genuine moral stance and is acting only in conformity with duty. The only way to avoid this is to render the will the originator and the author of the moral conduct that has been delineated up to now. This leads Kant to introduce his notion of the *autonomy* of the will of rational beings. Thus:

> Autonomy of the will is the property of the will by which it is a law to itself (independently of any property of the objects of volition). The principle of autonomy is therefore: to choose only in such a way that the maxims of your choice are also included as universal law in the same volition (G, IV: 440, 89).

The autonomous will is contrasted with the heteronomous one, which is regulated by laws external to it. "The will in that case does not give itself the law; instead the object, by means of its relation to the will, gives the law to it" (G, IV: 441, 89). Yet, given that acting on moral principles is not only a self-regarding activity but also one that concerns other people, autonomous self-legislation is at the same time legislation for other similar wills. How can the autonomous will avoid the danger of suppressing other wills in its legislating activity? Kant at this point asks his readers to participate in a thought experiment and to imagine a *kingdom of ends* (*Reich der Zwecke*), that is a community of law-governed rational beings, which is at the same time a community of objective and subjective ends. It can be viewed as a state of affairs in which all the ends achieved are not only compatible but are mutually supported to the extent of forming some sort of organic unity (Wood 1999, 166). In this community each rational will is bound by the moral law it imposes on itself, without being subject to any external pressure or any other form of interference, and it recognizes that the same holds for every other rational will. This is why it invests every rational being or person with dignity (*Würde*) conceived of as an absolute worth that is not open to trade-offs of any kind.[15] This commonality of autonomous wills and the artificial absence of divisive differences become the ground for fundamental equality and mutual respect that characterize their interaction. Hence when a rational will is legislating for itself, it is as if it is legislating for all through the universality of its law. But when we have to deal with finite human beings, this activity of the will should take the form of an imperative:

> [A]ct only so that the will could regard itself as at the same time giving universal law through its maxim (G, IV: 434, 84).
> Or
> [A]ct in accordance with the maxims of a member giving universal laws for a merely possible kingdom of ends (G, IV: 439, 88).

For Kant the three formulations of the categorical imperative are the expressions of the one and only objective and universal moral law. "There is nevertheless", Kant notes, "a difference among them, which is indeed subjectively rather than objectively practical, intended namely to bring an idea of reason closer to intuition (by a certain analogy) and thereby to feeling" (G, IV: 436, 85-86). Thus the first formulation focuses on the *form* of our maxims by demanding that we want them to become universal law; the second specifies their *matter* by asking that, when acting on our universalizable maxims, we treat rational beings as ends in themselves since this is what is required by the moral law, and the third offers a *complete determination* (*vollständige Bestimmung*) of our maxims by prescribing that these are to be chosen by an autonomous will which endorses universal moral law—as if it were a member of the kingdom of ends—and becomes at the same time irrevocably subject to it. Kant maintains that the first formulation is the most appropriate for the appraisal of moral judgments but adds that, if we want to "provide access" to the moral law, our maxims should comply with all three formulations.

Kant has now finished with the description of his novel metaphysical moral framework. It remains to defend it vis-à-vis other moral doctrines, such as those which locate the origin of morality in God's will or in an inner moral sense. The latter are dismissed in a few paragraphs as heteronomous or vague.

1.2.3. Third part. How are categorical imperatives possible or what is the ultimate condition of Kant's ethics?

In the third part of the *Groundwork*—the most enigmatic and controversial of all—Kant takes up the unanswered question concerning the possibility of categorical imperatives and seeks their ultimate condition. As we have seen, our actions are devoid of genuine moral worth if we lack an autonomous will. In the best of cases a moral law that is foreign to our will would make us act in accordance with duty but this formally correct moral stance would not arise from us. But are we autonomous in a morally interesting sense?

For Kant one way to tackle this tantalizing issue is to take the idea of *freedom* as given and derive the idea of morality from it. If the will is free, it is autonomous and thus it can be a self-legislating member of a kingdom of ends. Then it can will its maxims to become universal laws for all persons.

This approach, however, does not satisfy him. The notions of freedom and a self-legislating will are co-terminus and each one can be easily replaced by the other. Consequently, we could explain the self-legislating will through freedom and freedom through the self-legislating will. In other words we would be trapped in a vicious circle (G, IV: 450, 97).

The way out of this deadlock is to see the problem from a different perspective that draws on the distinction he elaborated in the *Critique of pure reason* (CPR, A 249/B 305 ff.): between things as they appear to our senses (*phenomena*) and things as they really are (*noumena*). Kant assumes that behind appearances there is another world that is not accessible to the senses. This is the realm of things in themselves, which are objects of pure understanding unable to be known through the categories. He now claims that when we apply this dichotomy between a sensible and an intelligible world to ourselves, we understand that behind our senses and feelings there is a self-constituting ego. With the aid of reason with which we are endowed we can think of ourselves as participating in these two worlds. Our membership in the sensible world makes us realize that we are subject to the laws of nature. Our membership in the intelligible world allows us to conceive of the operation of our will in no other way than under the aegis of *freedom*. It furnishes us with the opportunity to think that our will is determined by the special laws of the intelligible world and to cognize its autonomy "along with its consequence, morality" (G, IV: 453, 100). Thus:

> with the idea of freedom the concept of *autonomy* is now inseparably combined, and with the concept of autonomy the universal principle of morality, which in idea is the ground of all actions of *rational beings*, just as the law of nature is the ground of all appearances (G, IV: 452, 99).

If we participated only in the intelligible world, it would be natural and easy to follow the moral law; if we participated only in the world of appearances, we would be heteronomous and under the rule of various uncontrollable internal and external natural forces. Nevertheless, as we participate in both of them, we *ought* to follow the moral law and this is why it is stated in the form of a categorical imperative. The part of our will that is under the influence of the sensible world interacts with its counterpart that belongs to the intelligible world and, as "the world of understanding contains the ground of the world of sense and so too of its laws" (G, IV: 453, 100), we acknowledge the legislative authority of the latter over the former. This is attested to by the fact that even wicked persons, who are under the grip of their instincts and inclinations, would wish to live by the ideals of morality.

Yet as members of the intelligible world, we can only *think* of the idea of freedom. We can conceive of it *negatively* as independence from the laws of nature and the internal forces that determine our be-

havior as natural beings. Moreover, we can conceive of it *positively* but only as associated to the ability to invest our maxims with the universal validity of law (G, IV: 458, 104). What we cannot do is tell how this freedom is possible or offer an explanation of the way it works. Reason is unable to grasp the special and immutable laws of the intelligible world that govern the operation of the autonomous will in the sensible world. And, of course there is nothing analogous in the natural world, which is governed by its own different laws.

Kant summarizes his answer as follows:

> Thus the question, how a categorical imperative is possible, can indeed be answered to the extent that one can furnish the sole presupposition on which alone it is possible, namely the idea of freedom, and that one can also see the necessity of this presupposition, which is sufficient for the *practical* use of reason, that is, for the conviction of the *validity of this imperative* and so also of the moral law; but how this presupposition itself is possible can never be seen by any human reason (G, IV: 461, 106).

However, in the second *Critique* a significant change occurs. The order is reversed and now the possibility of categorical imperatives and of morality in general is not revealed to us through an analysis of the idea of freedom, but instead freedom is deduced from the moral law. Kant seems to recognize that from an epistemological point of view he cannot easily go from a negative account of freedom (freedom from the constraints set by the laws of the sensible world) to a positive account of it (freedom to act according to the laws of a supersensible world).[16] He appears to have second thoughts as to whether our mere thinking of an order that is different from the natural order warrants our cognizance of the "formal condition" of this intelligible order, namely the universality of the maxims of an autonomous will. (G, IV: 458, 104). On the other hand, a purely negative conception of freedom would be too weak and vague to make categorical imperatives possible.

> I ask instead from what our *cognition* of the unconditionally practical *starts*, whether from freedom or from the practical law. It cannot start from freedom, for we can neither be immediately conscious of this, since the first concept of it is negative, nor can we conclude to it from experience, since experience let us cognize only the law of appearances and hence the mechanism of nature, the direct opposition of freedom (C, V: 29, 163).

If the freedom solution proves epistemically problematic, then it is better to start from something given and not subject to further justification, the moral law, which bestows not only possibility but also reality to positive freedom and its special causality.

> It is therefore the *moral law*, of which we become immediately conscious (as soon as we draw up maxims of the will for ourselves), that first offers itself to us and, inasmuch as reason presents it as a determining ground not to be outweighed by any sensible conditions and indeed quite independent of them, leads directly to the concept of freedom (C, V: 29, 163).

Reason gives us the moral law and this is something that is presented to us as a self-evident a priori fact.

> Consciousness of this fundamental law may be called a fact of reason because one cannot reason it out from antecedent data of reason, for example from consciousness of freedom (since this is not antecedently given to us) and because it instead forces itself upon us of itself as a synthetic a priori proposition that is not based on any intuition...(C, V: 31, 164).

In addition, the authoritative fact of the a priori moral law now allows us to take the reality of the intelligible world seriously.

> The moral law...provides a fact that points to a pure world of the understanding and, indeed, even *determines* it *positively* and lets us cognize something of it, namely a law (C, V: 43, 174).

But by what thread of reasoning are we to arrive at the concept of freedom? We can start with the notion of "ought" of which we have a clear grasp. If we pose next the question "why ought we...?", we realize that the answer is not to be found in the world of experience. "The *ought* expresses a species of necessity and a connection with grounds, which does not occur anywhere else in the whole of nature. In nature the understanding can cognize only *what exists*, or has been, or will be" (CPR, A547/B575, 540). Therefore, for Kant the answer should be sought in the realm of pure reason. Only then does the practical character of it, that is the necessity to subsume our maxims to the universal moral law, become evident. However, this is not the necessity of the inexorable laws of nature from which we cannot escape. On the contrary, it is up to us whether or not to comply with the moral law. According to Kant we can exercise our power of choice (*Willkür*) and disregard the moral law for the sake of our inclinations, or we can show freedom of choice and endorse the moral law. For Kant freedom as a distinctively human quality is not freedom to act as we wish but to act morally, and this freedom is revealed to us when we are engaged in serious moral thinking.[17]

However, although from an epistemic point of view the moral law precedes freedom (*ratio cognoscendi*), from an ontological point of view freedom is the cause (*ratio essendi*) of moral law. Without it the idea of moral law would never have made its presence felt on us (C, V: 5, 140). Freedom in a positive sense (*positiv betrachtet*) constitutes one of the postulates of pure practical reason (C, V: 132, 246). This implies that it is a fundamental assumption that is taken as given and it is considered as an indemonstrable necessary condition of a priori practical reason (C: V: 122, 238). If we are able to act from the moral law, it is because we are free. Nevertheless, the mechanisms of this unique non-temporal causality of freedom are beyond our reach.

In concluding this section we could assert that categorical imperatives are possible because through them only pure practical reason makes manifest to rational beings like us the inherent in it moral law. Freedom and autonomy are necessary but indemonstrable presuppositions of the lawgiving function of reason. This is all than can be said without taking the risk of transcending our epistemic limits. In the words of one commentator, Kant's treatment of reason can be described as his Copernican revolution in ethics. "No one before Kant had thought to suggest that human reason could be so powerful" (Sullivan 1999, 44).

1.3. Morality, happiness and God

Despite certain views to the contrary, Kant is a philosopher who has much to say on happiness.[18] Happiness is something we all desire, but when we embark upon its pursuit, the results are often disappointing. This is due to the fact that we restrictively identify happiness with the achievement of a particular goal of ours such as becoming wealthy or successful only to discover in due course that this is not what we were looking for. Hence happiness becomes an endless and frustrating quest for new goals. Kant himself calls for a more holistic account of happiness and understands it as signifying a permanent state of overall satisfaction (*Wohlbefinden*) which results from the meeting of our needs, the realization of our inclinations and the fulfillment of our desires. The absence of any discrepancies between our volitions and the way things are is of paramount importance here as follows from the definition he puts forward:

> *Happiness* is the state of a rational being in the world in the whole of whose existence everything goes according to his wish and will, and rests, therefore, on the harmony of nature with his whole end as well as with the essential determining ground of his will (C, V: 124, 240).

Regarding its moral appraisal, Kant maintains in the *Groundwork* that the pursuit of happiness cannot be granted the status of a *moral principle*, for people are instinctively concerned with their own happiness, whereas the moral law is a priori and prescribes forms of behavior that run counter to our instincts and inclinations. In addition, happiness should under no circumstances be considered as an *incentive* to proper conduct. We have to act morally because our will recognizes the motivating influence the supreme ground of morality, the moral law, exercises on it and not because we expect to have pleasant feelings or to achieve some self-regarding goal.

However, in the second *Critique* Kant strongly supports a combination of morality and happiness surely not in the sense that morality is a means to happiness, but in the sense that moral persons *deserve* to be happy.[19] He introduces the idea of the highest good (*summum bonum*) by which he means that our moral stance should be accompanied by a degree of happiness strictly analogous to it. This combination, however, of the two terms is not synthetic, since it cannot have an empirical origin. Besides, it is not difficult to think of virtuous people who are not happy and the idea of happiness as an incentive to moral action has been ruled out. Neither it can be analytic; the concepts of morality and happiness are too heterogeneous to have one derive from the other. Thus Kant opts for an a priori synthetic solution by assuming the practically necessary existence of God, who, as the intelligent, omnipotent, omniscient and all-beneficent creator of nature, makes the highest good possible. "Only if religion is added to it [i.e. to morals] does there also enter the hope of some day participating in happiness to the degree that we have been intent upon not being unworthy of it" (C, V: 130, 244). God's existence cannot be demonstrated or cognized by other means but from a practical viewpoint it is rational to believe in it. Thus God becomes another postulate of pure practical reason. Moreover, to have serious hopes of attaining the highest good, our soul must be immortal, since during the limited time of our bodily presence in the world we cannot but make little progress towards a complete conformity with the moral law. The immortality of the soul is the third and final postulate of practical reason.

Kant has been criticized for preparing the ground for religious faith and for retreating from positions he forcefully argued for in the *Critique of pure reason*. [20] This is not the place for a discussion of his views on religion, which should include a careful study of his *Religion within the boundaries of mere reason* (1793). Nevertheless, if one adheres to the text of the second *Critique*, one gets the impression that God is "made" to fit perfectly into Kant's moral system. It is explicitly stated that God does not belong to speculative reason but to morals (C, V: 140, 252); that the divine commands are the laws of every free will (C, V: 129, 244); that God's will is holy in the sense that it does not need the necessitation of "ought" to act morally; and that by being subject to the moral law He is not the source of moral values as most religions proclaim (C, V: 131, 245-46). As to the possibility of knowing God, Kant not only dismisses it unequivocally but also maintains that it is a good thing that we do not have direct knowledge of His presence, since if we could prove God's existence, our actions would be done out of fear and resemble those of puppets (C, V: 147, 258). All these are facts that have to be taken seriously in addressing criticisms of this kind.

A final remark—Kant's effort to reunite morality and happiness brings him somehow closer to the ancient Greek ideal of *eudaimonia*, which roughly included not only hedonic feelings but also virtuous actions and possibly the presence of certain external goods. However, while this unity was self-evident for the ancients, for Kant it requires the intervention of a transcendent being to be achieved. Regardless of our views about the solution offered, most of us would agree with his diagnosis of the fragmentation between morality and happiness. Kant once more proves to be an archetypical philosopher of modernity.

1.4. *The metaphysics of morals* as a sequence to the *Groundwork*

In this rather neglected work Kant moves from the abstract level of the analysis and justification of categorical imperatives to the more worldly level of clarifying our duties. In the first part of the book, the *Doctrine of right*, he examines the a priori principles of external laws and the duties deriving from them. In the second part, which is closer to the subject matter of this chapter and is entitled *Doctrine of virtue*, he focuses on the ethical duties of the inner freedom of the will and offers a systematic classification of them as well as a specification of their content. In addition, he shows a strong interest in the practical presuppositions of acting from duty and this is why he emphasizes the notion of virtue and the forms of education required for the establishment and dissemination of this core idea of his moral doctrine. For Kant virtue means more than a disposition to do good deeds out of habit; it implies tranquility of mind and is conceived of as an inner strength that tunes the whole of our existence to follow the moral law.

> [V]irtue is not to be defined and valued merely as an *aptitude* and...a long-standing habit of morally good actions acquired by practice. For unless this aptitude results from considered, firm, and continually purified principles, then, like any other mechanism of technically practical reason, it is neither armed for all situations nor adequately secured against the changes that new temptations could bring about (MM, VI: 383-84, 515-16).

Returning now to the classification of duties, Kant makes various distinctions such as between duties of right and duties of virtue—where the criterion is whether they can be expressed through external legal rules—duties to oneself and duties to others and so forth (cf. the table presented in Sullivan (1989, 70-71)). No other distinction, however, has given rise to such philosophical controversies as his distinction between *perfect* and *imperfect* duties.

Perfect duties are absolute and prescribe specific forms of action that have to be performed strictly without any deviation or adjustment on the part of the agent. For instance no one is allowed under any circumstances to kill herself for then she destroys her own humanity and morality, which she ought to protect (MM, VI: 423, 547). But the most debatable of Kant's perfect duties concerns truth telling. In his essay "On a supposed right to lie from philanthropy" (1797) he holds that the duty of truthfulness is "a sacred command of reason prescribing unconditionally, one not to be restricted by any conveniences", even in cases in which a lie is necessary to deceive a determined prospective murderer (L, VIII: 427, 613). Here we can distinguish two claims. The first is about the general disvalue of lying and throughout his work Kant

offers various arguments in support of this claim. For example, he argues that the liar debases herself, that she uses other people merely as means or that generalized mendacity would thwart one's desire for knowledge. The second claim concerns the absolute prohibition of lying and the underlying rationale is that any compromise of absolute principles in the form of legitimate exemptions would "nullify the universality on account of which alone they are called principles" (L, VIII: 430, 615).[21]

On the contrary, imperfect duties specify only maxims of action, are susceptible to exemptions (but only if the agent has to perform another overriding duty), and leave us sufficient leeway for acting according to our best judgment. Failure to perform them does not necessarily betray malice, but possibly lack of moral strength or mistaken judgment. One example is our duty to make other people happy which requires some sacrifice on our behalf. But "[h]ow far it should extend depends, in large part, on what each person's true needs are in view of his sensibilities, and it must be left to each to decide this for himself." This duty "has in it a latitude for doing more or less, and no specific limits can be assigned to what should be done" (MM, VI: 393, 524). Another example is the duty of self-perfection, which demands the cultivation of our natural and moral powers. Here the fact that our efforts to cultivate our talents depend significantly on external circumstances in conjunction with the non-negligible possibility to form the wrong picture about the purity of our own moral agency make any attempt to offer a detailed description of self-perfection prohibitive (MM, VI: 392-93, 523).

The study of *The metaphysics of morals* is indispensable for a fair treatment of Kant's practical philosophy. It helps to keep the right perspective in regard to the standard objection that his ethics constitutes a closed formal system that is insensitive to the needs, desires and goals of real people. If we remain at the level of the specification of duties this complaint loses its bite. It is impossible to promote anybody's welfare if you are not really concerned about this person.[22] Of course this does not make Kant a follower of what we now call an "ethic of care", but considerations to that effect are not altogether missing from his writings. In addition, in the same work it becomes evident that Kant now takes a strong interest in the popularization of his moral ideas. He makes up a dialogue, "a fragment of *moral catechism*" in his words, between a teacher and a pupil in which the former, exercising Socratic midwifery, extracts from the latter the idea that we have to act from duty without expecting anything in return (MM, VI: 480-82, 593-95).

This two-page dialogue constitutes the simplest and most concise exposition of Kant's moral philosophy.[23]

The metaphysics of morals is important for one more reason: it shows that Kant is aware of the moral/non-moral distinction and is convinced that only a part of human behaviour should be subject to moral appraisal. He speaks of a fantastically virtuous person (*phantastisch-tugendhaft*) who pokes her nose into other people's lives and judges every aspect of them from a moral point of view. The problem with this person is that she refuses to admit that there are morally *indifferent* things. Kant castigates this attitude on the ground that it can render the power of virtue tyrannical (MM, VI: 409, 536).

At this point the introductory account of Kant's ethics comes to an end. Every effort has been made to present his views in a charitable spirit, to highlight the unity, originality and richness of his moral thought and, to pinpoint certain criticisms of it that, in my opinion, are not supported by adequate textual evidence. It is now time to maintain a certain distance from Kant and to pass to the main argument of the essay.

Notes

1. For instance, one common misunderstanding is that Kant's ethics is formal in the sense that it can accommodate even morally abhorrent maxims insofar as they can pass the test set by the first formulation of the categorical imperative. This view is apparently endorsed by John Stuart Mill (1861/1998, 51-52) when he says of Kant that "when he begins to deduce from this precept [the first formulation of the categorical imperative] any of the actual duties of morality, he fails, almost grotesquely, to show that there would be any contradiction, any logical (not to say physical) impossibility, in the adoption by all rational beings of the most outrageously immoral rules of conduct". This is not true, since, as we shall see below, the first formulation of the categorical sets significant limitations on maxims approved, and, more importantly, it is a mistake to see it in isolation from its other formulations.

2. For an excellent account of the novel elements Kant brought to the moral philosophy of his time, see Schneewind (1998, esp. chaps. 1 and 23). For a brief description of his influence to posterity, see Höffe (1994, chap. 13).

3. To be precise, Kant here is expressing his doubts concerning the establishment of a "perfectly just civil constitution".

4. There are also the posthumously published *Lectures on ethics*, a text based on the notes taken by Kant's students who attended his courses at the Albertina University in Königsberg. However, in my view, references to the *Lectures* should be made with caution and only to provide additional evidence or further elaboration for positions stated in the works the philosopher published when alive.

5. The bibliography on Kant's ethics is immense. Some recent general influential works are Baron (1995 and 1997), Herman (1993), Hill (1992), Korsgaard (1996), O' Neill (1989), Sullivan (1989) and Wood (1999). The collective volumes edited by Guyer (1998), Höffe (2002) and Timmons (2002) can serve respectively as companions to the study of the *Groundwork*, the second *Critique* and *The metaphysics of morals*.

6. For specific methodological similarities between Kant's ethics and his epistemology, see Cassirer (1981, chap. 5). However, it should be pointed out that when it comes to practical matters, Kant takes great pains to allow the possibility of beliefs that are for him epistemically unfounded. Speculative or pure reason has to accept as practically necessary certain (non-contradictory) propositions of practical reason, even if it cannot have any cognizance of them. For Kant the practical aspect of reason takes precedence over the theoretical.

7. Later Kant will endorse the point of a reviewer that he (Kant) did not put forward a new principle of morality but only a new formula of it (*Formel*). And he would hasten to add that this is not of lesser importance, since his for-

mula does in ethics what formulas generally do in mathematics, namely they "determine what is to be done to solve a problem" (C, V: 8, 143).

8. "Even if, by a special disfavor of fortune or by the niggardly provision of a stepmotherly nature, this will should wholly lack the capacity to carry out its purpose...then, like a jewel, it would still shine by itself, as something that has its full worth in itself" (G, IV: 394, 50).

9. In the second *Critique* Kant will add that this will can serve as a model, which human beings can "only approximate" (C, V: 32, 166).

10. "Nature" here does not refer the natural world but to a state of affairs that is regulated by laws. Nature thus conceived is described as "the *existence* of things, insofar as that existence is determined according to universal laws" (P, IV: 294, 89).

11. For a synopsis, see Baron (1997, 64-76). Nevertheless, if I were to make only a small comment concerning the current debate, I would distance myself from the tendency to think of the first formulation tout court as a handy recipe that is intended by Kant to provide answers to all questions regarding moral decision-making.

12. I suppose that the underlying principle here is "if you want to follow your feelings and act accordingly, do not do things contrary to your feelings". Along similar lines, one can reject the maxim of gratuitous self-mutilation: bodily integrity is a precondition for maximum self-control.

13. If domination is a form of exploitation, then it is easy to understand why the maxim that the powerful should dominate the weak cannot become a universal law. This particular maxim could also be criticized for the reason that it is against a rational agent's best interests to believe in it, if she thinks she belongs to the camp of the weak or is aware of the eventuality of becoming one of them.

14. This term was coined by Joel Feinberg and it is discussed in Feinberg (1986, chap. 17).

15. In the second *Critique* it becomes evident that the respect we owe to other people is eventually due to their observance of the moral law (C, V: 76-78, 202-3). In addition, once the will gives itself the moral law, it becomes subject to it in the sense of acknowledging the law's superiority (C, V: 82, 206). This presumably means that the autonomous will is not allowed to have second thoughts on its choice of the moral law and to decide to reject its supreme authority.

16. As Allison (1990, 227) puts it: "Kant refers to both a Verstandeswelt [a world of understanding] and a intelligibilen Welt [an intelligible world]...and he slides from the former to the latter without sufficient justification. The former is to be understood negatively as encompassing whatever is nonsensible or 'merely intelligible', that is, whatever is thought to be exempt from the conditions of sensibility...The latter is to be understood positively as referring to a

supersensible realm governed by moral laws, a 'kingdom of ends' or equivalently 'the totality of rational beings as things in themselves'...".

17. Kant gives an example to illustrate his position. He mentions a man whom the sovereign threatens with death if he (the man) fails to give false testimony against an honest man the sovereign wants to destroy. Kant maintains that the very fact that this person considers the possibility not to submit to the will of the sovereign and to suffer the consequences of his refusal unveils a form of freedom that would be inconceivable for him in the absence of the moral law (C, V: 30, 163-64). For the distinction between *Wille* and *Willkür*, see MM, VI: 213-14, 374-75.

18. For a recent thorough and fair discussion of Kant's conception of happiness, see Hill (1999).

19. The argument is deployed in the second chapter of the second *Critique* (V: 110-33).

20. One example is Heinrich Heine, who claimed that "[b]y this argument Kant distinguished theoretical from practical reason and, as with a magic wand, brought to life the corpse of deism which theoretical reason had killed" (quoted by O' Neill (1997, 270)). In the same essay O' Neill offers a detailed rebuttal of these criticisms that draws on a variety of Kant's texts.

21. I extensively discuss Kant's views on lying in Peonidis (1994), where I argue that the first two formulations of the categorical imperative do not condone its absolute prohibition.

22. Thus our wish "not only to be treated as a person—any person—but to some extent to be treated as the particular persons we are" (O' Neill 1989, 111) is not being neglected when the happiness of others as an end becomes a duty.

23. For his approach to moral education, see Herman (1998).

Chapter two

Towards a post-Kantian moral image

2.1. Maintaining distances from Kant

"Fifty years ago", William A. Galston (1993, 207) observes, "the influence of Kant's moral and political philosophy extended scarcely further than a few German professors and their disciples. Today, evidence of Kant inspired practical philosophy is pervasive." It should be noted that this influence is not limited to an acknowledgment of his historically significant contribution to the shaping and evolution of concepts and conceptions that concern us—such as autonomy or deontological ethics—but it makes its presence felt in a more creative manner in representative works of major contemporary philosophers. It is as if many of these philosophers consider it necessary to appropriate something from his legacy and to establish links with his thought. Thus Nozick (1974, 28-33) furnishes a Kantian justification for his core idea of rights as side-constraints. Habermas (1993, 1) maintains that his own discourse ethics is part of the Kantian tradition. And above all Rawls, a philosopher who is the driving force behind this current revival of the interest in Kant's practical philosophy, points out that the principles of justice as fairness can be seen as categorical imperatives and envisages his pivotal assumption of citizens as free and equal persons as deriving from an elaboration of Kantian autonomy (Rawls 1973, 251-57). Even philosophers belonging to the opposing utilitarian camp such as R. M. Hare (1997, chap. 8) feel the urge to write essays to show that Kant *could* have been on their side.

However, many of those philosophers who pay tribute to Kant at the same time emphasize that certain of his positions cannot form part of a current normative account. There is no consensus as to which these are, since even the most counterintuitive Kantian tenets have their modern defenders. I believe, however, that the list that follows summarizes certain plausible objections that can here and now be raised against his moral doctrine. These criticisms do not count as refutations in a strict sense of the term, given that disproving a philosophical position requires more than expressing doubts about its validity or believing the truth of its opposite. It is rather that these objections reflect the changes that some of our constitutive and more or less intuitive beliefs have undergone through the passage of time, with the result of becoming incongruous with certain basic Kantian assumptions and positions.

First, at a normative level it is difficult to accept that there are perfect duties. It is not impossible to think of cases in which even killing is morally permissible or even required, for example in self-defense, and the same holds for lying and suicide. Our reluctance to opt for moral absolutism comes from our conviction that we have to deal with an infinite variety of complex moral situations in which various conflicting values are at stake. Our inability to think of all the possible cases to which a maxim or a duty applies constrains us from arguing that we should always respond in the same way.[1]

The argument about the heterogeneity of values has been brilliantly expressed by Thomas Nagel:

> Just as our understanding of the world involves various points of view—among which the austere viewpoint of physics is the most powerfully developed and one of the most important—so values come from a number of viewpoints, some more personal than others, which cannot be reduced to a common denominator any more than history, psychology, philology, and economics can be reduced to physics. Just as the types of understanding available to us are distinct, even though they must all coexist and cooperate in our minds, so the types of value that move us are disparate, even though they must cooperate as well as they can in determining what to do (Nagel 1979, 138).

The problem is that all these values cannot always cooperate in the same way. Different situations may lead to different value orderings and trade-offs. This makes us confront moral absolutism with cautiousness but it does not necessarily make us act-utilitarians or subjectivists. We can assign priority to certain of our principles, rules or maxims because we deem them of paramount moral importance while allowing them to be outweighed by other values in carefully considered, exceptional cases.

Second, in Kant's practical philosophy we encounter many remnants of substantive metaphysical thought that can hardly gain our acceptance at a time when there is a considerable demand for "public" accounts that can be formulated in less controversial and more universally accessible terms. What allows us to believe in the distinction between phenomena and noumena? How is it possible for two completely different and incompatible forms of causality—the mysterious causality of freedom and the well-documented causality of the laws of nature—to act simultaneously in the world of appearances? Can the immortal soul approach moral perfection without entering different bodies? Is reincarnation a fourth postulate of practical reason? But perhaps, as has been pointed out a long time ago, the most serious problem is the highly abstract and idealized setting in which the discussion of categorical imperatives (but not the specification of our duties) reaches its completion. The device of a kingdom of ends inhabited by rational beings from which all individual differences have been wiped out is too far removed from the concerns, priorities and considerations of ordinary people. It is not only that we may not be motivated to act as if we were members of a kingdom of ends; we do have reasons *not* to do that, since, in the words of an eminent commentator, "acting in this world by rules designed for another can prove disastrous" (Hill 1992, 66).[2] Thus it appears that the device of the kingdom of ends has to be abandoned in favor of a more down-to-earth moral approach that is closer to the real world of human affairs. This is a move that produces not only gains but also losses.

Third, Kant's understanding of autonomy diverges significantly from our own. There is no doubt that his phrase that an autonomous rational being "is not to be subjected to any purpose that it is not possible in accordance with a law that could arise from the will of the affected subject himself" (C, V: 87, 210), if it is taken out of context, could easily serve as a slogan for promoting a modern conception of autonomy. It expresses the widely accepted idea that respect for someone's autonomy means, among others things, not preventing this person from being the author of her own decisions. However, a great deal of caution is needed here. Kant is apparently the first modern philosopher who ascribes supreme value to autonomy, but it should not escape our attention that he restrictively identifies it with voluntarily subjecting oneself to the moral law that is innate in rational beings. This is why in the *Groundwork* autonomy is understood as choosing maxims that can become universal laws and it is made the "sole principle of morals" (G, IV: 440, 89). But this is *not* the way we conceive of autonomy. For us an autonomous person is someone who is in charge of her life and tries to resist any external intervention or internal constraint that hinders her in the exercise of this invaluable function. This in no sense implies that the autonomous person necessarily makes decisions based on moral reasons, let alone Kantian moral reasons. Although it is evident that a genuine moral stance presupposes autonomy, given that only legality but not morality can be institutionally enforced, the opposite does not hold. Someone can autonomously decide to opt for gross immorality and accept the consequences (if any). For Kant, as stated in the first chapter, this is out of the question.[3]

Fourth, the claim that the moral law is a fact of reason is hardly satisfying. Kant apparently takes for granted that the moral law is something that is revealed to each individual rational being and makes its imperatives known through a process of self-reflection. But as Bittner (1989, 89 ff.) observes, this is an ad hoc solution not supported by argument. The only thing that can be said to those who doubt the existence of the moral law is that they refuse to recognize an obvious fact. To this skeptics can always respond that it is natural to refuse to see something that it does not exist, and the discussion comes to a standstill. As to the argument that even wicked people would wish to live by the ideals of morality, the skeptic's reply is that this wish does not corroborate the existence of the moral law, for it may be due to the fact that these people too live in societies in which moral conduct is publicly valued. If we are to accept or reject a moral fact of reason, we need stronger evidence than that provided by Kant.

This leads to a critical investigation of Kant's conception of the nature of practical reason and its capacity to be the only motive for doing what it prescribes. Starting with the second issue, one can ask what the motivating power of practical reason means for us. It is reasonable to assume that it amounts to an internal urging to do x only because we understand that x is vested with the authority of reason. From this it does not follow that we will necessarily do x, as our final decision may be dictated by non-rational factors such as a compulsion to avoid x. Nevertheless, even in cases like the above, the urging to do what reason demands presents itself forcefully in our deliberative process. This qualification is necessary to avoid attributing to the supporters of the motivating power of practical reason the highly demanding view that rational persons unfailingly follow the precepts of reason. It suffices for rational persons to have strong motives generated by reason, although its motivational influence may not always be decisive in determining deliberation or action.

The next issue one has to consider concerns the content of practical reason, that is the specification of the commands it forces upon us. As aptly suggested by Korsgaard (1996, chap. 11), we cannot argue for or against the motivating power of practical reason before deciding what practical reason is about. We first have to reach agreement on the rational character of a certain precept and then inquire if it suffices to make us act accordingly. And this holds even for philosophers like Hume, who maintain that reason can only provide us with the means for fulfilling our ends.

My point is that there are widely acceptable commands of reason that are motives, but these do not include the categorical imperatives of Kant's practical philosophy. More specifically, many people would affirm that it is rational to seek the most efficient means to carry out their plans and this affirmation triggers in them the motive for doing so. If they realize that someone does not want, ceteris paribus, to use the most efficient means to her ends, then they will either characterize her stance as irrational or form the impression that she does not in fact desire to pursue her professed ends. Moreover, for most people it is prima facie rational to promote their own interests and to a certain extent the interests of their kin and this motivates them to a sufficient degree, although in the end they may act otherwise.[4] Once again (along with Kant) they consider someone who consistently and persistently acts as if she has absolutely no personal interests irrational, and in particular if she for no obvious reason neglected the most fundamental of them, self-preservation. Finally, I would be willing to grant that there are morally significant forms of conduct—in the sense that when generalized, they become collectively beneficial—which are rational and capable of motivating us. For example, many would agree that it is rational to be cooperative in their everyday transactions or not to request things that cannot be done. Yet the significance of these rational considerations regarding the moral authority of reason and its motivating force should not be overestimated. Firstly, we can endorse these considerations moved by purely prudential reasons. Secondly, here it does not suffice to acknowledge the rational character of these precepts to be motivated by them; we also need a great deal of empirical information about the particular situation we are dealing with. Thus, based on our perception of the situation, it is not unusual to decide to be uncooperative or to make claims we know cannot be satisfied. The upshot is that the motivating force of these rational but not necessarily moral considerations is considerably weaker than the other two types of rational considerations mentioned above and this is due to our reluctance to bestow even a prima facie absolute validity on them.

We can now return to Kant and to his two basic positions that are relevant to the issue in question: (a) that pure practical reason "announces itself as lawgiving" by providing human beings with the moral law and (b) that this law constitutes the sole acceptable motive for the will.[5] The final question that arises is whether we grant practical reason such a heavy and commanding content.[6] Do we assign, for example, the categorical imperative to act upon universalizable maxims the same rational necessity we assign the hypothetical imperative to learn the alphabet if we want to become educated? The answer is "no". We do not accuse someone of inconsistency or irrationality because she does not show respect for persons (Foot 1978, 161 ff.). In parallel, we do not perform our duties (including many of those proclaimed by Kant) because this is rational. Perhaps the world would be a better place to live if we believed that morality and rationality were just two sides of the same coin, but this does not happen. It is not that at a certain stage our deliberative process is underdetermined by non-rational factors, which eventually prevent us from being motivated by the moral authority of reason we unreservedly acknowledge; simply from the outset we do not locate the source of any categorical command to adopt the universal and impartial standpoint of morality in reason.[7] The preconditions for adopting this standpoint should be sought in a completely different context.

2.2. The post-Kantian moral subject

The purpose of the preceding discussion was to identify four controversial basic assumptions in Kant's moral philosophy that, in my view, should not be part of a workable normative account of Kantian origin or inspiration. Now I can proceed to an outline of such an account, which I shall call a *post-Kantian moral image*. However, before going into detail, something should be said about the meaning of the terms "moral image" and "post-Kantian."

A moral image is not a full-blown and exhaustive ethical theory starting with general principles and ending with a set of strict guidelines about what we should do in particular, morally-demanding circumstances. It does not claim to have an answer to every moral question. Neither does it endorse a descriptive approach to morality in the sense of identifying, monitoring and registering all those processes related to ordinary moral thinking and decision-making. On the contrary, I understand it as a comprehensive pattern of ethical thought that retains a high level of generality and aims to impose some order on our normative considerations. However, we should not expect too much from it, especially when it comes to the determination of the particulars of moral conduct. The most a moral image can offer is some clues about the fundamentals of ethics by shifting ethical reflection in a certain direction. Its appeal, if any, consists in putting forward a core justificatory framework the details of which are to be filled in by individual agents at their own risk. Moreover, for a moral image to stand a chance of being convincing, it has to be accessible to ordinary agents with no special training in philosophical ethics. This practically means that it has to be close enough to their actual concerns, priorities and pre-theoretical beliefs to the extent of requiring extensive adjustments of them but not a complete reversal of the agents' moral world-view.[8]

The expression "post-Kantian" means that the proposed moral image is inspired by and draws upon Kant's practical philosophy, while at the same time it avoids the aforementioned problematic Kantian positions and incorporates others that have been vehemently rejected by Kant.

Let us now imagine an individual who lives in a Western, democratic society and is not indifferent to moral issues. In particular our subject, who from now on will be called the "post-Kantian moral subject", is seeking some general ethical guidance that will help her in her decisions and evaluations. The only precondition she sets for her quest is not to rely as far as possible on religious, transcendent or metaphysical considerations and arguments. She is determined to take for granted only what she has direct experience of, either through self-reflection or through her interaction with other people. It has to be made clear in advance that I do not claim that people do subject themselves to the same deliberative procedure or that they would necessarily reach the same conclusions with the post-Kantian moral subject if they were involved in a similar pursuit. Everything that follows has a heuristic value. If some readers find that they can share the reasoning of our subject or that they could agree with the normative conclusions deriving from it, then the suggested moral image will gain plausibility; otherwise it would one more stillborn philosophical attempt at moral theorizing.

Through a process of self-reflection and self-observation, the post-Kantian moral subject discovers that she is capable of acting *autonomously*.[9] This ideally means that she is always able to carry out successfully plans of action that she has freely chosen (in a meaningful sense) and that enjoy her approval. Meaningful free choice presupposes the presence of a set of *dissimilar* and *substantial* possibilities for action, of which she decides to realize one, while she could (in the sense that it would not be physically impossible or highly improbable) have done otherwise. For instance, our subject does not possess substantial possibilities for action when caught in the horns of the dilemma "your money or your life", since based on our knowledge of human nature we assume that choosing death is not in all probability a real option for her. Along similar lines it can be argued that she does not have a meaningful choice when all her options are not seriously differentiated, as when she has to decide between two, equally alienating jobs.[10]

Approval concerns the control she exercises over her beliefs and desires that are involved in the formation and the execution of significant short-term or long-term plans of action. The autonomous subject takes a strong interest in the epistemic processes that result in having certain basic beliefs including moral beliefs. She scrutinizes their origins in order to re-examine and revise those she judges were brought about by distorting internal mechanisms (self-deception, bias and so forth) as well as those that are not backed by sufficient evidence or have been surreptitiously imposed on her by other agents (i.e. through propaganda or deception). She wants to know and endorse the reasons justifying her beliefs. Concerning her desires she takes great pains to dig out their causes and to obtain an assessment of the overall consequences of their fulfilment. For instance, she wants to know if the fear underlying her desire x is justified; or if she will not regret the changes the realization of her desire y will bring to the world. Once again, if she realizes that there is something wrong with the formation of her desires or that she does not desire the implications of their fulfilment, she is able without further ado to ignore or alter them.[11]

It should be made clear that what has been described up to now is an *ideal* form of autonomy the attainment of which would require extraordinary epistemic virtues, the ability to fully understand all of our mental activities and absolute self-control.[12] Moreover, it would presuppose that the world is tailor-made for us. None of these presuppositions apply and thus we have to focus on humanly *feasible* autonomy, which, due to the enormous diversity of human beings, is a matter of degree and is modelled on its ideal counterpart. I could say that the post-Kantian moral subject is adequately autonomous if she possesses a considerable range of options and the required abilities to carry out successfully some of her approved crucial plans of action, even if in the long run it turns out that all her actions were in fact determined by an evil genius or her genes. As far as approval is concerned, the way she is related to her beliefs and desires does not of course resemble the way a surgeon is related to the body of her patient, but the post-Kantian moral subject is not a puppet in the hands of others or in the grip of her urges either. Between these two extremes, and many setbacks and failures notwithstanding, there is an ample margin for humanly feasible approval of beliefs and desires.

There are also certain misconceptions pertaining to the notion of autonomy, which have to be clarified.[13] It is not uncommon to associate personal autonomy with an individualistic approach that envisages people as self-sufficient, independent and pro-social units. This implies that autonomy is an exclusively individual achievement. However, this is not true. It does not follow from the fact that someone makes and carries out plans of action that enjoy her approval that she has more possibilities of success if she acts on her own. On the contrary, some of her plans of action may be realized only through the concerted activities and efforts of many people. In other cases she has to take advantage of what others have already produced. The general point here is that feasible autonomy depends on certain conditions that can only be provided by a proper socio-political environment. For instance, the critical and reflective capacities needed for the control of our beliefs and desires can be developed and stabilized only through carefully-designed, educational intervention, and an open democratic society that provides its members certain basic goods, services and opportunities supports this autonomous agency in ways that are unthinkable in autarchic societies or in societies in which the population lacks the bare essentials. Not to mention the obvious fact that many natural impediments to the exercise of our autonomy are removed through the concern and the expertise of specialists such as physicians or trainers. The development and exercise of autonomy depends considerably on the cultural milieu, and it would not be far from the truth to contend that someone who grew up outside society would be less autonomous than someone of a sane mind who had spent most of her adult life locked up in a dungeon.

It is also believed that the autonomous person conceives and pursues only novel ideas and ideals or that she comes up with highly original and uncommon plans of action. However, autonomy "need not require that one be the ultimate source of one's desires and values, but only that one have the capacity to assess them critically" (Reath 1998). Besides, inventiveness and originality, whenever they become manifest, presuppose the endorsement of many pre-existing background assumptions. The feasibly autonomous person is influenced from various sources just like everyone else, but she does not accept them unquestionably. Perhaps, after reflection, she might feel satisfied with widely acceptable and commonplace views and ideas. Her world might not necessarily be a new world, but it would be her *own* world.

Next, the post-Kantian moral subject realizes that autonomous agency in the above sense is of paramount importance to her. Why is this so? First, it makes her feel that she is the architect of her life and that she assumes responsibility for it. It enables her to discover what is of real value to her. It makes her enjoy not what she likes but what she, after reflection, wants to like in the circumstances given. But it is more than this. As an autonomy theorist points out "autonomy is not just a means to contentment, since one may be content without being autonomous" (Young 1986, 26) or, I would add, autonomous without being content. The point is that even if our subject fails to carry out her autonomously-chosen plans of action, even if she later decides they were not worthy of her efforts, or even if she does not manage to overcome her biases or phobias, she has tried to leave her trace upon the world instead of being a passive receiver of external stimuli and this very fact has intrinsic value for her. The actual process of autonomous thinking and acting, the mere fact that she strives to follow choices backed by her own considered (or reconsidered) beliefs and desires gives meaning to her life. Autonomy is not only valued for what it makes us achieve, but for its own exercise irrespective of outcome. If we lose it completely, this "would be like a light going out" (Haworth 1986, 185).

I have made the assumption that the post-Kantian moral subject is adequately autonomous and that she ascribes intrinsic and instrumental value to her autonomous thinking and acting which is compatible with an immense variety of plans of action.[14] Is this a contrived or far-fetched assumption that jeopardises the cogency of the moral image discussed? I think many people would find it plausible as autonomy in the sense of reflective self-governance or self-determination is highly valued and cherished far beyond the confines of academic philosophy.[15] In the twentieth century it became evident that the manipulation of the masses (including the allegedly, more weary intellectuals) was easier than one had expected. At a macro-level we witnessed the unprecedented support many totalitarian regimes enjoyed through exploiting their subjects' weak points and by relying heavily on a meticulously orchestrated, state propaganda; at a micro-level we have studies and experiments demonstrating that ordinary persons under certain conditions develop a tendency to perform reprehensible actions if these people are commanded to do so by a recognized authority (military, scientific or otherwise), actions that they would never have thought of performing if they were acting on their own.[16] But even in democratic, consumer societies, ordinary citizens are bombarded by so many alluring external stimuli (many of which are deceitful and dictated by financial and partisan political interests) that they run the danger of progressively losing their epistemic and volitional independence. The mass media and advertising now have at their disposal formidable techniques for patronizing people's thought and action. Thus the need to form autonomous individuals, who would dare to use their mind and resist efforts of manipulation and thought control whatever their origin, is widely recognized. This need has been highlighted by Kant and other major figures of the Enlightenment, but only recently have we come to realize the full impact of this legacy.

Finally, in her everyday dealings with other people the post-Kantian moral subject discovers that other people think and act more or less as autonomous agents as well, and this is a matter of paramount importance to them. However, this discovery does not provide her with a motive to respect their autonomy whatever this means. An appeal to reason would not help much, since, as previously stated, the most reason can do is urge her to care about her personal autonomy or (perhaps) the autonomy of a handful of people with whom she already has relations of intimacy. From a purely rational standpoint, she has neither reason nor motive not to abstain from affronting other people's autonomy insofar as she has nothing to gain in terms of the promotion of her own personal autonomy.

What is needed for genuinely valuing other people's autonomy or for acknowledging the *moral* value of autonomy, is an *emotional* substratum that would motivate her accordingly. An emotional substratum should enable her to approach others, to find out what evil has befallen them and to try to do something for their own sake without expecting any sort of pay-off. At this point we have to enter the realm of emotions and see them in a more favourable light than Kant and traditional logocentric moral philosophy. In particular, I will maintain that our moral subject shows respect for other people's autonomy because she is capable of *sympathetic* concern. Yet if this claim is to have any substance, it has to be backed by a detailed account of the nature and the value of the moral emotion of sympathy. Thus the deployment of the post-Kantian moral image will be postponed until this account is given and this will be the subject of the next chapter.

Notes

1. For Kant conflict of duties cannot arise. He admits only to the possibility of conflicts between grounds of obligation and if a conflict of this sort occurs, then the stronger ground prevails (MM, VI: 224, 378-79). Nevertheless, Kant's moral absolutism needs one more premise that we can hardly accept: that the stronger ground of obligation in a particular case retains the same strength in every case imaginable. For a cogent critique of moral absolutism, see Rachels (1997, chap. 9).

2. The same author in a more recent work (1997, 23-27) expresses his reservations about Kant's commitment to the idea of people who choose as isolated entities based on their personally invented values since this approach downplays the historical, social and cultural dimensions of value choices. His remarks remind us of the well-known Hegelian objection that Kant in fact relies on, without admitting it, the pre-existing rightness or lawfulness of institutions such as property (or promising) and this happens because practical reason is unable to justify or reject them (Hegel 1802-1803/1975, 77-78). Yet I would rather claim that Kant understands that all values cannot be created ex nihilo by solitary rational beings. He attempts to remedy this problem by establishing some communal moral bonds through membership in the kingdom of ends, but his solution is too fictitious to be a workable one. Cf. note 4 in this chapter.

3. Cf. the various conceptions of autonomy discussed in Johnson (1994, 71-77) and O' Neill (2002).

4. As seen, the kingdom of ends is viewed as a systematic union of rational beings from which all individual differences and private aims have been removed. This conception could give rise to the following interpretation: in the kingdom of ends each rational subject has achieved such a high degree of unity and commonality with other rational beings that her own good is at the same time everyone's good. Thus the rational personal interest she has in pursuing her own good could be re-described as universal lawgiving. Even if we accept this interpretation for the sake of argument, this derivation of Kant's normative principles from rational self-concern still lacks any motivational force. When it comes to the world of ordinary human beings, in which conflicts of interests, scarce resources, competitive relations and mutually incompatible ends abound, self-concern does not by definition entail concern for others.

5. "Now if by an *incentive* (*elater animi*) is understood the subjective determining ground of the will of a being whose reason does not by its nature necessarily conform with the objective law, then it will follow...that no incentives at all can be attributed to the divine will but that the incentive of the human will (and of the will of every created rational being) can never be anything other than the moral law" (C, V: 72, 198).

6. I think it is not unfair to Kant to appeal to a commonsense understanding of practical reason to challenge his own conception of it. As previously

stated, Kant was convinced that he was reconstructing and justifying widely shared moral beliefs.

7. Bernard Williams (1985, chap. 4) has pointed out that when we seek truth guided by theoretical reason we adopt an impartial point of view, since we consider that if x is true, it must be true for every rational being. This does not happen when we are engaged in practical deliberation since we do not consider it necessary to do what everyone would have reason to do or what would have everyone's approval. Perhaps in the final analysis, reason might not possess the unity that Kant wanted it to have.

8. I borrow the term "moral image" from the writings of Hilary Putnam and Dieter Henrich who actually refer to a "moral image of the world". According to Putnam (1987, 67) "a moral image...is not a declaration that this or that is a virtue, or that this or that is what one ought to do; it is rather a picture of how our virtues and ideals hang together with one another and of what they have to do with the position we are in. It may be as vague as the notions of "sisterhood and brotherhood"; indeed, millions of human beings have found in those metaphors moral images that could organize their moral lives..." For Henrich (1992, chap. 1) a moral image of the world amounts to the totality of dominant empirical and metaphysical assumptions that accompany a subject's moral beliefs. He offers as an example the previously mentioned Kantian postulate that happiness should be proportional to moral conduct. It goes without saying that the conception of a moral image offered by Putnam, who depicts it as a cohesive idea capable of somehow tidying up our moral lives, is more relevant to the one explained above than Henrich's.

9. The account of autonomy that follows draws heavily on an earlier work of mine (Peonidis 1994, 195-214). However, I now realize that in *Lying and morality* the transition from autonomy as a prudential value to autonomy as a moral value was left unexplained. I hope here to make up for this crucial omission.

10. Here I follow Raz's (1986, 373-77) analysis of "adequacy of options" as a condition of autonomy.

11. For a detailed account of the various aspects of belief control, see the discussion of what Mele (2001, chap. 5) calls "doxastic self-control". The idea of approving our desires as part of autonomous choice and action owes much to Frankfurt's (1971) influential suggestion that a person enjoys freedom of the will when her second-order volitions (I want to want to x) are in line with her first-order volitions (I want to x). This notion of approval is what distinguishes autonomy from liberty "which is conceived either as a mere absence of interference or as the presence of alternatives" (Dworkin 1988, 107).

12. For ideal autonomy, see Haworth (1986).

13. Cf. the relevant remarks of Crittenden (1993) and Reath (1997).

14. Many philosophers seem convinced that the only incompatible plans of action are those that in all probability would cause permanent damage to an agent's capacity for autonomous thinking and acting. They think of consensual

slavery or various forms of self-inflicted harm ranging from self-mutilation to drug addiction. Nevertheless, although the above examples are quite telling, I would take this position with a grain of salt. What I have in mind are cases in which a single, autonomously-made decision is of such importance to a person that she is willing to sacrifice everything for the sake of it, including her capacity to make autonomous decisions in the future.

15. Indeed it not accidental that one of the most eloquent defenses of autonomy is to be found in Peter Weir's film *The Truman Show* (Paramount Pictures 1998).

16. I am thinking of Milgram's (1974) experiments concerning obedience to authority and of Haritos-Fatouros (2002) study on the shaping of torturers' identity in Greece and Brazil.

Chapter three

Sympathy as a moral emotion

3.1. Kant again

According to a strong philosophical tradition that was inaugurated with Plato and—if we take his autobiography at face value—cost John Stuart Mill a period of depression, emotions (the passions of the ancients) are classified among the darkest elements of human nature. They are located at the antipodes of reason and undermine its operations; they are unreliable, blind, passive, subjective, and often lead to harmful or inappropriate action. Hence if we cannot eliminate them, we have to keep them under the constant control of our higher mental qualities such as reason or the intellect. This is not regarded as an impossible task. As Descartes (1650/1985, 348) put it, "even those who have the weakest souls could acquire absolute mastery over all their passions if we employed sufficient ingenuity in training and guiding them".[1]

However, many of the assumptions comprising this demeaning account of the emotions are no longer valid thanks to modern interdisciplinary research. Emotions are now viewed as evaluative reactions of the mind to certain external stimuli. These reactions are considered essential for acknowledging our own weaknesses and needs (or those of others) in our effort to understand adequately and cope successfully with a world which is to a significant degree beyond our control (Nussbaum 2001, Ben-Ze'ev 2000). The emergence of emotions involves cognitive processes. In many cases emotional reactions have a "cognitive antecedent" such as when I try to find out whether the person "stamping on my foot in the subway did so intentionally" (Elster 1996, 1387). Moreover, they may be neither at the antipodes of reason nor its major opponents, given that they can act as substitutes to rational procedures or be enmeshed in them. They limit, for example, "the range of information that the organism will take into account" as well as the set of its options by indicating what is "salient among its objects of attention". Consequently, they help the organism to frame the problem she has to deal with and thus facilitate decision-making in ways the rules of reason cannot do (de Sousa 1990, chap. 7). It is also possible that our physiological make-up is such that there is a closer connection between reason and emotion than was thought in the past. According to an influential hypothesis:

> The lower levels of the neural edifice of reason are the same ones that regulate the processing of emotions and feelings, along with the body functions necessary for an organism's survival. In turn these lower levels maintain direct and mutual relationships with virtually every bodily organ, thus placing the body directly within the chain of operations that generate the highest reaches of reasoning, decision making, and, by extension, social behavior and creativity. Emotion, feeling, and biological regulation all play a role in human reason (Damasio 1994, xiii).

Generally speaking there is an emerging consensus that emotions contribute in various significant ways—that need further investigation—to not only our survival but also our well-being. This by no means implies that emotions cannot betray us on certain occasions. Wanton emotional outbursts or the display of emotions that are inappropriate for a given situation can have harmful consequences for the agent or the persons affected by her behavior. Thus the need to control our emotions as far as possible remains one of the few common points between the traditional logocentric approach and its modern interdisciplinary counterpart. However, whereas in the former the regulation of emotions was left to reason and/or the virtues, in the latter this role is assigned to *emotional intelligence*. It is a form of intelligence different from the one measured by IQ tests and, according to its major proponent, its object is the recognition and control of our emotions, the understanding of the emotions of others, the finding of motives for ourselves and the successful handling of interpersonal relations (Goleman 1988).

To be sure, this is not the place for a general discourse on the emotions. The sole purpose of the preceding remarks is to point out that, despite significant disagreement and controversy, emotions are now seen rather favorably and have ceased to be the scapegoat of philosophical anthropology or moral psychology. This core background consideration paves the way for a positive evaluation of the moral function of sympathy or compassion that will occupy us in this chapter.[2] But before proceeding to this it is appropriate to clarify the significance of the above emotion in Kant's practical philosophy.[3]

If we confine ourselves to the *Groundwork* and the second *Critique*, the picture we get of sympathy is rather dismissive. Sympathy is conceived of as an inclination of empirical origin and as such does not possess genuine moral value and can never constitute an acceptable motive for moral action. It is likely to make some agents act in conformity with duty but never from duty (G, IV: 398, 53). Its absence is absolutely inconsequential for normative deliberation and decision-making as these are guided by practical reason and not by emotions. Neither can its presence be of any positive value for at least two reasons: (a) sympathy is volatile and thus can disappear as soon as the agent is overwhelmed by her own personal problems and (b) if it precedes the appropriate procedure for the determination of moral duties, it spreads confusion to the agent, who wants to get rid of its influence and submit only to the authority of pure practical reason (C, V: 118, 235). No matter how gentle and refined an inclination is, it never ceases to be "blind and servile".

This picture undergoes significant changes as we shift our attention to *The metaphysics of morals*. As noted before, here Kant is more concerned with the practical aspects of his moral doctrine and thus develops an interest in the more empirical (or anthropological) issue of the role of non-rational factors in ordinary duty-based conduct. In discussing the imperfect duty to love other human beings, Kant claims that love is not to be conceived of as a feeling but as a maxim of benevolence (*Wohlwollen*) (MM, VI: 449, 569). This rational and active benevolence, which is defined as "satisfaction in the well-being (*Wohlsein*) of others" (MM, VI: 452, 571), should be strengthened through a particular duty of humanity (*humanitas practica*) that envisages man as a psychosomatic entity. This duty is described as willingness and ability to share in others' feelings but only in an active and disciplined manner that protects us from being "infected" by the grief and pain of the sufferers, especially when there is nothing to do for them (*humanitas aesthetica*).[4] No one is to gain by such useless dissemination of pain. What is required is not to share in the feelings of others and to wish them well but to perform our duty to "sympathize actively with their fate".[5] This duty can be achieved through an indirect duty to

> cultivate the compassionate natural (aesthetic) feelings in us, and to make use of them as so many means to sympathy based on moral principles and the feeling appropriate to them. –It is therefore a duty not to avoid the places where the poor who lack the most basic necessities are to be found but rather to seek them out, and not to shun sickrooms or debtor's prisons and so forth in order to avoid sharing painful feelings one may not be able to resist. For this is still one of the impulses that nature has implanted in us to do what the representation of duty alone might not accomplish (MM, VI: 457, 575-76).

But what cannot be achieved by the representation of duty alone and in what exactly does the contribution of compassion lie? Here the text is not very informative and so it is necessary to make certain hypotheses that would be consistent with Kant's overall moral doctrine. Presumably, compassion cannot be an *additional motive* for performing our duty to love other human beings, given Kant's explicit statement that even well-meant adulterations of the motivating power of the moral law with other incentives are deemed as manifestations of humanity's natural propensity to evil (R, VI: 29-30, 77-78).[6] Then, what is its function? Why should someone who has no special professional or personal reasons frequent hospitals and prisons? I will assume that compassionate feelings can be beneficial in three different ways. First, in the *Groundwork* Kant speaks of a "judgment (*urteilscraft*) sharpened by experience", which is necessary for a priori law to decide where it is applicable (G, IV: 389, 45), and we know that for him judgment signifies "the faculty of thinking the particular as contained under the universal" (CJ, 5: 179, 18). Now an agent who can sympathize with other people in the way described by Kant becomes familiar with various forms of actual human suffering, most of which are unknown or incomprehensible to an indifferent person, and this accentuates the critical power needed to apply general principles successfully to particular cases. Second, the cultivation of compassionate feelings may prevent the emergence of emotions that are harmful to others such as envy, malice or resentment thus doing a great service to the will in its effort to comply with the moral law. Third, a compassionate moral agent may be more easily disposed than an agent who does not experience this emotion to perform her duties pleasantly.[7] However, one way or another sympathy or compassion as a pure emotion has only a secondary and auxiliary role limited to the application of moral principles. It is entirely excluded from the process of the justification of these principles and it can never serve as a motive of moral action.

3.2. The nature and value of sympathy

Although sympathy as a moral emotion figured prominently in the works of major thinkers of the past such as Hume, Adam Smith, Rousseau and Schopenhauer, until recently it had not attracted the attention of most twentieth-century philosophers (with the exception of Max Scheler). One reason for the revival of philosophers' interest in sympathy appears to be the ongoing systematic and interdisciplinary effort to give a psychological or biological answer to the old conundrum about humans' selfish or altruistic nature. The philosophical history of sympathy and other cognate terms is long and perplexing. If one would like to identify a common element in terms such as *sympathy*, *compassion*, *empathy*, *fellow-feeling*, *pitié*, *commiseration*, *Mitleid* or *Mitgefühl*—employed by diverse philosophers in different contexts— perhaps this could be the distress or the sorrow we feel vis-à-vis the pain or misery of others. However, this consideration is hardly sufficient for constructing a modern, functional conception of sympathy.

The first thing to note is that sympathy is a *primitive* emotion in the sense that it cannot be explained in terms of other emotions (Taylor 2002, 3). Second, it should be conceived as a *genetically endowed mechanism* that precedes socialization. Thirdly, sympathy is *intentional*, meaning that it is about something (Elster 1996, 1387). The intentionality or aboutness of emotions distinguishes them from feelings (pains and itches do not point at something external to them) and according to Ben-Ze'ev (2000, chap. 3) it can be broken down into three simpler elements: the cognitive, the evaluative, and the motivational. The first element refers to the information necessary for understanding the situation the subject faces, the second concerns the significance this information has for her, and the third her desire to react appropriately. To these should be added a fourth element, the "feeling component", which describes what the subject feels when she experiences a particular emotion.

Now if the aforementioned analysis is applied to sympathy, the cognitive element in it amounts to the subject's perception of people (or other living creatures) of whom she has direct or indirect experience. The evaluative element concerns her consideration that the person observed is in distress or suffering. However, this consideration does not come as the conclusion of a long, deliberative process that involves complex and abstract principles or theories but "it is based upon ready-made structures or schemes of appraisal which have already been set during evolution and personal development" (Ben-Ze'ev 2000, 58). Thus at first sight the subject assumes that someone is suffering not based on a particular religious or moral doctrine it happens to espouse, but simply because she sees this person to be in pain or in danger, to be unable to meet certain basic needs and function normally, to be treated like an animal, to be shocked, sad, miserable and so forth. The motivational element in the case of sympathy consists in the subject's willingness to do something for the sufferer. Here the gamut of her reactions could range from a simple word of comfort to self-sacrifice. Finally, the feeling component describes the discomfort, the embarrassment or the displeasure the subject feels when confronted with someone's suffering. A typical example of the experience of this emotion is the case of a Dutch resistance fighter who, during an allied bombardment in WW II, rescued a wounded German soldier saying afterwards that at this moment he "saw simply a human being in need" (Taylor 2000, 7-8).[8]

To these it should be added that the manifestation of sympathy does not depend on whether its recipient is aware of her dreadful situation. As Adam Smith put it long ago:

> We sometimes feel for another, a passion of which he himself seems to be altogether incapable; because, when we put ourselves in his case, that passion arises in our breast from the imagination, though it does not in his from the reality (Adam Smith 1759/1984, 12).

He held that sympathizing with a joyful but mentally ill person amounts to imagining how we would be feeling if we were in her position and could have an objective assessment of our condition. However, to remain close to our analysis, here it could be asserted that our sympathy is simply due to the fact that this person has lost her sense of reality, something we regard as a symptom of mental illness.

Finally, a few words should be devoted to sympathy's cognate, the widely-discussed concept of *empathy*, although the picture one gets from the relevant literature is far from clear.[9] According to a contemporary psychological definition, "empathy is the ability to 'live on the inside' (*embiosis*) the situation of another person, the ability to understand and share in his emotions, thoughts and behaviour" (Malikiosi-Loizos 2003, 296). From this definition it follows that empathy could be compatible with the absence of a motive to assist the person whose negative feelings, emotions and thoughts we "are living on the inside" or re-enact with the help of our imagination. For instance, I can feel what it is like for you to be jealous of me, but this is not necessarily accompanied by a desire to help you get rid of this unpleasant emotion. In this sense the experience of empathy is not a *sufficient* condition for sympathy. Moreover, and here Kant would apparently concur, it is not a *necessary* condition either (Blum 1980, 510, Goldie 2000, 213-19). Fortunately, we do not have to identify with someone (or "to imagine ourselves in someone's shoes") to feel sympathy for this person.[10] Under certain circumstances this identification is impossible, such as when a man observes the pain and agonies of childbirth; under other circumstances it is unnecessary, as in the case of the Dutch resistance fighter who sees the wounded enemy soldier faltering. This does not mean that someone who has the gift of projecting herself into other people's mental states may not develop the tendency to sympathize with them more easily or that, from an evolutionary or psychological standpoint, there is no affinity between empathy and sympathy. It is just that empathy has no place in the conceptual analysis of sympathy defended here.

What is the moral value of sympathy?[11] I claim that sympathy contributes to the endorsement of moral values and principles and to their practical application in a positive and constructive manner. Someone who is already touched by other people's plight, who shows compassion for the needy and the distressed without much thought and without expecting anything in return, who feels like a member of the family of man can more easily adopt and act upon abstract and universal principles, such as respect, happiness, non-maleficence or beneficence.[12] As Nussbaum (2001, 388) points out "the good of others means nothing to us in the abstract or antecedently. It is when it is brought into relation with what we already understand...that such things start to matter deeply". And what we already understand (at least some of us) is the compassion we feel for certain people we interact with. On the contrary, if we are indifferent to human suffering or, even, worse, experience in advance only negative emotions towards our fellow human beings, then what moral motives could we have for ascribing people, say, basic inalienable rights? Of course, once through the mediation of sympathy an agent reaches a threshold in which she starts thinking in terms of universal moral principles, she does not need to feel sympathy for every individual she interacts with, guided by these principles. Someone may impeccably perform her duties to persons for whom she feels no sympathy.[13] It would be far-fetched and perhaps unrealistic to takes sides with

Schopenhauer (1841/1998, 144) in proclaiming: "only insofar as an action has sprung from compassion does it have moral value". My point is simply that it is difficult for an ordinary person to become motivated to perform her duties to *everyone* else, if she is not already emotionally predisposed to do something to alleviate the suffering of those who come to her attention (Mercer 1972, Gill 2000). To put it figuratively, sympathy sets in motion the cogs and wheels of moral conduct.[14]

However, sympathy's moral value is not exhausted in its contribution to the endorsement of moral principles. Even if it does not pave the way for systematic and reflective moral reasoning, the manifestation of sympathy is prima facie valued in itself since by definition it is exemplified in forms of altruistic behavior. This holds even in cases when the sympathetic agent eventually fails to do anything substantial for the sufferer. "Even when nothing can be done by the compassionate person to improve the sufferer's condition, simply being aware that one is an object or recipient of compassion can be an important human good" (Blum 1980, 515). Yet, from the assumption that sympathetic concern has prima facie moral value, it does not follow that any action done out of sympathy has an all-things-considered value. An agent may have a mistaken conception about the good of other people; she may be quite selective in expressing her sympathy thus refusing to see that there are other individuals who urgently need her attention or she may show compassion for the wrong person (as when someone who is fully aware that a person is a dangerous criminal helps that person out of sympathy). This is why most authors recognize the limitations of sympathetic concern and insist that it should be supplemented or offset through the acceptance of a wider moral perspective which includes an objective conception of the human good or, alternatively, universal principles of justice, equality and desert.

It should be emphasized that the above account of the moral value of sympathy differs significantly from the Kantian one, which assigns to sympathy only an (unclear) auxiliary role in the *application* of moral principles. On the contrary, here it is argued that the emergence of sympathy in the sense described has prima facie intrinsic moral value, since it implies altruistic behavior, and that it is a necessary precondition for acknowledging a principled moral framework.

3.3. Empirical findings

The discussion of the nature and value of sympathy could have ended here. Yet, the fact that one is dealing with a moral emotion and not with a moral principle creates an additional explanatory burden. A philosopher who defends an abstract moral principle or a regulative ideal can easily assert, as Kant has done, that it retains its value intact, even if no one ever endorses this ideal. Nevertheless, a philosopher who bases morality on a particular emotion cannot make a similar claim. If no one experiences this emotion or if it does not exist in an elementary natural form that could be cultivated through moral education, then its value is negligible. In our case this means that if people are incapable of feeling sympathy in the sense described, the preceding discussion becomes meaningless; it is as if one is professing the value of walking on water. It is therefore necessary to present some empirical evidence concerning the emergence and the nature of this emotion. From the time when Butler was arguing against Hobbes' psychological egoism, philosophers have managed to come up with a few telling examples of admirable and presumably altruistic behavior, like the one of the Dutch resistance fighter. However, the evidence provided by single examples is hardly sufficient. More systematic research is needed to show, if possible, that the "moral heroes" of the above examples do not act the way they do guided by various prudential reasons. This research has been done by contemporary psychologists and I now turn to their work by positing two crucial questions: "What is the psychological basis of sympathy?" and "Can we ever know with certainty that there are no selfish motives behind actions seemingly done out of sympathy?".[15]

Concerning the first question, Martin L. Hoffman's (2000, esp. chaps. 2 and 3) work on the developmental process of empathy in childhood is illuminating. First, he identifies five mechanisms—ranging from the involuntary and automatic to the most controllable and cognitively demanding—which make the arousal of empathy possible. Children can feel as others feel because they imitate their facial expressions, they respond to conditioned stimuli, they evoke their own unpleasant experiences when they observe people in distress, they understand verbal communications describing unpleasant situations and they can imagine themselves in the position of other people. Next he discerns five stages in the development of empathy:

a) *Newborn reactive cry*. The starting-point of this process is the cry of newborns when they hear other infants crying.

b) *Egocentric empathic distress.* At this stage one-year-olds react similarly but less passively when they observe other children in painful situations, still without being able to distinguish their own distress from the others' distress.

c) *Quasi-egocentric empathic distress.* Here children, who are a few months older, start making comforting but clumsy, non-verbal advances toward children in distress, while they continue to fail to understand the distinctiveness of the others' position.

d) *Veridical empathic distress.* Now toddlers, having become more self-conscious, gradually start taking the role of other people they observe and this makes them more efficient helpers.

e) *Empathic distress beyond the situation.* At this final stage, the beginning of which has not yet been determined, children can sympathize with the overall situation of the person in distress (including her past and future) and not only with its directly observable elements (facial expressions, etc.). This enables them to feel empathic distress for persons who are absent and to identify with disadvantaged groups. It is important to notice that Hoffman (2000, 87-88) makes it clear that as soon as children are able to distinguish their distress from the distress of others, "the motive to comfort themselves is correspondingly transformed into a motive to help the victim...From then on and continuing into adulthood...children want to help because they feel sorry for the victim, not just to relieve their own empathic distress". Thus the last stage in the development of empathy can be seen as a precursor to our definition of sympathy and thanks to Hoffman's scheme we have a plausible (but presumably not a final) account of the psychological origins of sympathy.

In regard to the second question, one can appeal to the significant empirical findings of the social psychologist Daniel C. Batson, which seem to make a case for the non-selfish character of sympathetic agency. These findings are part of a long-term research project whose objective is to control the "empathy-altruism hypothesis," that is the assertion that the experience of empathy evokes altruistic motivation. In his writings *empathy* is defined as "one particular set of congruent vicarious emotions, those that are more other-focused than self-focused, including feelings of sympathy, compassion, tenderness, and the like" (Batson 1991, 86); and *altruism* is meant as a "motivational state with the ultimate goal of increasing another's welfare" and not (a) of avoiding the unpleasant and embarrassing feelings the agent experiences in the sight of the victim's suffering (what in psychological jargon is called "aversive arousal reduction"), or (b) of getting some personal benefit (or avoiding some burden) (Batson 1991, 6 and passim.). Thus described his empathy-altruism hypothesis is close enough to the conception of sympathy defended in this essay so it would not be inappropriate to refer to the results of his experiments, keeping in mind that in these experiments people are observed under artificially-induced and controlled conditions.

The general pattern Batson follows in his studies consists of asking one group of participants to try to imagine what a person in distress is feeling, while a second group of participants is called upon to treat the same individual in an objective and aloof manner. Batson makes the assumption that people belonging to the first group will tend to be more altruistically orientated compared to those of the second group, and the results of his studies seem to corroborate this assumption.[16] In regard to our question, Batson quite plausibly considers that if the subjects act altruistically only to reduce aversive arousal, then they would have no reason to act in this manner if they were free to leave the scene without any repercussions. To find out whether this was true, he conducted (among many others) the following experiment (Batson 1991, chap. 8): his associates asked female psychology undergraduates to observe through closed-circuit television a young woman, Elaine, who was supposed to suffer slight electric shocks periodically, while she was performing a simple task. Half of the students (the low empathy group) were asked to evaluate the situation as objectively as possible, while the other half (the high empathy group) were instructed to try to sympathize with Elaine. All participants were also informed that, due to a past traumatic experience, Elaine might overreact even to mild shocks. Next the experimenters told the first half of the first group to observe only a part of this embarrassing process and then to leave the room, while the second group had to stay until the end of it. The second group received exactly the same instructions. Then at a certain stage of the procedure the experimenters gave all the participants the opportunity to replace Elaine and suffer the shocks themselves. The result of this experiment was that 91% of the first half of the high empathy group, namely the students who could easily leave the room, volunteered to take Elaine's place. This result strengthens the assumption that altruistic behavior, at least on certain occasions, is not evoked by a desire to escape from an embarrassing situation but from the emotion of sympathy (Batson's empathy). Similar experiments by the same researcher showed that altruistic behavior does not originate from a desire to avoid sanctions or to acquire benefits.

It is not my wish to claim that these findings are unanimously accepted among psychologists or to discard the possibility that the same agents may act differently in real-life situations. There is no doubt that we are only at the beginning of a long process of discovery, but I believe that the evidence supplied is sufficient to grant that sympathy exists in more than just the philosophical imagination.

However, apart from research in developmental and social psychology, a careful look at certain recent political and social events bears witness to the existence of sympathy, as well as to how easily it can be manipulated. Those who propagate racism and xenophobia are aware that they are unable to achieve their aim by appealing to reason. They focus on the sympathy we feel for other people and try to make us believe that members of foreign races and ethnic groups are not entitled to our compassion, since they are inferior to us. Nazi training did not consist of imposing the idea that the extermination of the Jews was a requirement of an a priori moral law but, instead, that Jews were "subhuman", "viruses" and "vermin" who did not deserve the compassion of the Aryans. Showing this emotion was considered as a weakness, as something not becoming of a Nazi (Glover 2001, chap. 35, Nussbaum 2001, 424), and unfortunately many wholeheartedly endorsed this view. The problem is that racism continues to attract supporters because through carefully designed intervention our emotional moral make-up can be suppressed or become blind to the sufferings of strangers. However, there might be some good news in this story. If our moral emotions, and sympathy in particular, can be manipulated to serve racism and bigotry with relative success, why should they not be cultivated to serve nobler purposes? The fact that in the eighties many Westerners were mobilized not by arguments but by the pictures of starving African children should not escape our attention. Moral emotions can be shaped, developed and given direction, and this quality that they possess offsets the traditional charge that they are blind and unreliable (Oakley 1993, chap. 4).[17]

Now I will use the conception of sympathy sketched here as a catalyst for proceeding with and completing the post-Kantian moral image.

Notes

1. For an informative outline of various aspects of the logocentric tradition, as well as the ways of dealing with the unruly emotions in ancient Greek thought and in Descartes, see Cottingham (1998, esp. chaps. 2 and 3).
2. In this essay I will use these two terms interchangeably.
3. For detailed discussions of sympathy's role in Kant's moral philosophy, see Baron (1995, chap. 5) and Sherman (1997, chap. 4).
4. Cf. the distinction drawn in *Anthropology* (A, VII: 236, 104) between sensitivity and sentimentality. Sensitivity is the ability to control the impact of positive and negative feelings on us, while sentimentality is our inability to resist becoming the passive recipients of other people's misery.
5. Cf. a similar discussion in the *Lectures on ethics* (LE, XXVII: 419-22, 181-84) in which Kant criticizes those who merely wish other people to be happy without doing something about it. Showing sympathy for someone amounts to contributing to the pursuit of her happiness or to the alleviation of her pain.
6. Baron (1995, 220) points out that the prohibition to adulterate incentives concerns only perfect duties and not imperfect ones, such as the duty of love. However, in the above passage Kant unambiguously condemns the idea of mixed motives as motives of actions done from duty, without alluding to any distinction or exception.
7. In *The metaphysics of morals* Kant makes it clear that moral action should not be regarded as a burden one has to bear but, instead, that it should be performed pleasantly and cheerfully (MM, VI: 484-85, 597-98).
8. Sympathy must be distinguished from two other relevant emotions: in *remorse* the agent is responsible for having wronged the person she sympathizes with, and in *pity* the agent feels sorry for someone but does not want to intervene on this person's behalf for a variety of reasons. For a detailed analysis, see Tudor (2001) and Ben-Ze'ev (2000).
9. For a clear distinction, see among others Chismar (1988). It should be noted, however, that the two terms are often used indistinguishably in the philosophical literature. Characteristically, Hume describes an empathetic mechanism when he says of sympathy: "The minds of all men are similar in their feeling and operations; nor can any one be actuated by any affection of which all others are not in some degree susceptible. As in strings equally wound up, the motion of one communicates itself to the rest, so all the affections readily pass from one person to another, and beget correspondent movements in every human creature... [Sympathy is the] principle which takes us so far out of ourselves as to give us the same pleasure or uneasiness in the characters of others, as if they had a tendency to our own advantage or loss" (Hume 1739-1740/2000, 368 ff.).

10. It is noteworthy that in her interviews with persons who behaved altruistically by risking their lives to save other people, Monroe (1996, 203-4) came to the conclusion that they lacked empathy for those whom they had rescued.

11. Concerning this question, the spirit of Max Scheler's (1912/1970) analysis is quite helpful, despite the fact that he eventually rendered love and not *Mitgefühl* the key notion of morality. For various contemporary defenses of the moral significance of sympathy, see Mercer (1972), Blum (1980), Oakley (1993), Vetlesen (1994), Darwall (1998), Goldman (1998), Gill (2000), Benze'ev (2000) Tudor (2001) and Nussbaum (2001). For an opposing view, see Goldie (2000). Recently, sympathy has been used by Crisp (2003) to defend a particular conception of distributive justice, which gives priority to the worse off, and Slote (2003) argued that certain crucial deontological distinctions (like the one between killing and letting die) have an empathic origin. It is my opinion that we will soon witness many endeavours to combine sympathy with basic moral principles.

12. This approach, in my opinion, bears mutatis mutandis certain similarities with the central Millian argument in the third chapter of *Utilitarianism* entitled "Of the ultimate sanction of the principle of morality". Here Mill seeks a natural sentiment that would lie at the basis of utilitarian ethics and that would motivate us, in conjunction with moral education, to recognize the happiness of the many as "the ethical standard". For him this sentiment is identified with the "social feelings of mankind", which are construed as the "desire to be in unity with our fellow creatures" (Mill 1861/1998, 77 ff.).

13. Nevertheless, we may be better *persons* if our principle-based judgments and our evaluative emotional reactions converge. On this, see Oakley (1993, chap. 2).

14. This position is weaker than the one maintained by Darwall (1998, 262) who suggests that "the concept of a person's good or well-being is one we have *because* we are capable of care and sympathetic concern". Someone may have a clear picture of the well-being of others and be completely unmotivated by it. My point is that without feeling sympathetic concern we are unable to recognize as valid any obligation whatsoever to pursue the good of others.

15. For a general psychological account of sympathy, see Wispè (1991). Readers might wonder why I do not turn to evolutionary biology for the required evidence. This is an issue that cannot be elaborated here and I will just mention two reasons. First, the explanations given by biologists who try to connect behaviour with reproductive capacity are a far cry from ordinary moral considerations and they are unlikely to be accommodated to a moral image. On the contrary, psychological explanations seem to square with our account better. Second, as Sober and Wilson (1999, 12) warn us, even if natural selection favours unselfish motives, this does not disprove psychological egoism. It is still possible for "nonselective processes to have blocked or reversed the effects of natural selection".

16. In addition, this assumption has been corroborated by studying a prisoner's dilemma structure in which participants had to choose between cooperation and non-cooperation in the context of an ordinary business transaction (Batson and Moran 1999). The result was that 70% of the participants—who were told only that the other person needed to be cheered up as well as to imagine how she felt—decided to cooperate thus taking the risk of receiving the worst possible payoff. This study is of paramount significance since it shows that sympathetically-motivated, altruistic behavior is possible even in settings in which people are expected to act motivated only by self-interest.

17. On the possibility of an institutional promotion of rational and controlled compassion, see Nussbaum (2001, chap. 8). The most outstanding among her suggestions are the implementation of egalitarian policies, the rejection of disgust as grounds for legal sanctions, the change in public attitudes concerning the vulnerable, the castigation of shame related to the natural decay of the body and the cultivation of the imaginative abilities of students through their exposure to literary texts.

Chapter four

Autonomic obligations

4.1. The image continued and completed

On the basis of the previous discussion I will make the reasonable assumption[1] that the post-Kantian moral subject feels sympathy (in the sense described) for the people she interacts with and this is something she approves of after reflection. She is moved by the plight of those surrounding her and she is motivated to act on their behalf. This moral emotion she now experiences has a profound impact on the way she conceives of the value of other people's autonomy.[2] Up to this point she has acknowledged the prudential significance it had for them, but she was not at all committed to show respect for it. However, from now on she realizes that persons around her suffer serious harms when their autonomy is assaulted, and this is something she does not want to happen. Thanks to sympathy she ascribes *moral* value to their autonomy as she does, say, to their health and safety. To be sure, it takes her more time to learn that the violation of their autonomy is seriously harmful compared, for example, to the violation of their bodily integrity, but the process of recognition is roughly the same. She is now genuinely concerned with the fact that those close to her desire to be the authors or the architects of their lives and this signifies for her a change in her other-regarding attitudes. However, her expression of sympathy need not be targeted exclusively to relatives, friends and other persons immediate to her. With the aid of imagination, reasoning and her knowledge of certain simple general facts about human nature, the post-

Kantian moral subject comes to recognize the moral significance of people she has never known or she will never meet. As a result of this process of sympathetic acknowledgment, she becomes disposed to do something to protect the autonomous thinking and acting not only of those forming her inner circle but also of other more distant persons she might affect with her acts and omissions.

Sympathy has now set in motion the cogs and wheels of the procedure leading to respect for individual autonomy, but it cannot finish the job without the aid of meticulous moral reasoning and deliberation. Thus, the post-Kantian moral subject seeks to determine what to do to show her concern for other people's autonomy in the most efficient way. One possibility she considers is to devote herself to the promotion of everyone's autonomy, but this is ruled out for a variety of reasons. Given the conflicting plans and projects of humans, her decision to help agent A to carry out plan x might prevent agent B from materializing plan y and vice versa. Nevertheless, even if human plans were always compatible, our subject would have to spend her whole life in serving the ends of everyone else. This is not a thrilling prospect for her. The autonomous post-Kantian moral subject has her own life plans, the pursuit of which might be valuable only to her (or a few others) and she does not intend to forego all her pursuits, although she takes into consideration the impact of her actions on her fellow humans. She is not a "moral saint" and thus she must give a different meaning to her sympathetic concern for others' autonomy.

Another possibility is simply not to interfere in any non-trivial sense with the lives of others and to let them think and act as autonomous persons. Nevertheless, after reflection she realizes that human interaction involves intervening in people's life plans and belief systems in ways that are not trivial but do not count as violations of autonomy. This happens, for instance, when through cogent arguments and without exercising any sort of pressure, we convince an adult of sound mind to quit her job, to get married or to become religious. Autonomous persons are not like Leibniz's monads and it would be unreasonable to contend that trying to change someone's mind without force of fraud betrays disrespect for that person's autonomy. In addition, the post-Kantian moral subject understands that under certain circumstances non-interference jeopardizes the autonomy of others. As we have seen in the second chapter, securing and promoting individual autonomy constitutes a common enterprise to a great extent and this commits our subject to participate in her capacity in it.

Hence she decides that her sympathetic concern for other people's autonomy should ultimately be expressed in the form of certain obligations she owes to every human being irrespective of any special relation, attachment or agreement. She understands that these obligations, which she considers binding for all persons endowed with sympathy, could be revised or supplemented through further reasoning, but she is convinced that their observance establishes a minimal general framework for the protection and respect of individual autonomy.

In particular she undertakes the following obligations:

-To respect human life and bodily integrity, since they constitute the conditio sine qua non of autonomous thinking and acting.

-To be truthful, since by deliberately misleading people she makes them establish an epistemically defective relation to their environment and often leads them to decisions they would not have taken if they had had true information. This is a clear attack on their autonomy.

-Not to resort to force and coercion, since forcing people to do what they do not want to do betrays gross disrespect for their autonomy.

-To be tolerant in the sense of not harming people merely because she does not agree with their views or with their (harmless to others) preferences and life-styles. She grants that if one does value autonomous thinking and acting, one has a prima facie obligation to respect what ensues from it as well, even if the final outcome appears epistemically unfounded, embarrassing or imprudent.

-Not to deprive others of the means necessary for the pursuit of their autonomously chosen plans (i.e. their property or their freedom of speech). In addition, she undertakes the positive obligation to contribute, in a manner suitable to her, to the long-term and onerous collective effort that aims to prepare the ground so that, eventually, everyone enjoys decent standards of living, everyone is offered equally distributed opportunities, and the entire range of one's civil, political and social rights is honored.

-Not to vilify other people simply on the grounds of race, ethnicity, religion, gender, sexual orientation or social status. Discriminating against people on one of these grounds means among other things that she deliberately destroys the self-respect, the self-confidence and the resolve people require for choosing and pursuing significant plans. All these forms of bigotry could be seen as malicious and unfounded denials of the autonomy of certain categories of persons.

Apart from the above provisional set of universal "autonomic" obligations, the post-Kantian moral subject is bound by "local" duties and commitments arising from particular positions and relationships she has voluntarily chosen or those within which she is embedded. These might be duties to family, friends, customers or colleagues. Here it need not be stressed that these duties might include more than respect for autonomy as, for example, she is expected to care for the happiness or the well-being of her children. However, autonomic obligations have normative priority for our subject. This means that she is not allowed, as a matter of principle, to violate the autonomy of a total stranger in one of the aforementioned ways to maximize the happiness of her family. Her additional local obligations, whatever they are, cannot be discharged at the expense of her universal autonomic obligations.

From this point onwards the moral image becomes deliberately blurred as our subject tries to act according to the autonomic obligations she has voluntarily undertaken. In her effort she is burdened by significant difficulties, which are partly due to the complexity of the situations she has to deal with—and the variety of morally salient features she has to take into consideration each time—as well as to the unfortunate fact that others do not always comply with autonomic obligations. As a result she is led to acknowledge that in practice these obligations should be subject to reasonable exceptions. Tolerance has its limits, some forms of coercion may be justified and the prohibition of lying cannot be absolute. The problem is that she is not always certain where to draw the line and on what grounds. Of course she tolerates the expression of dissenting political beliefs but she is not convinced that this implies suffering financial damages because most of the time the town center is inaccessible due to demonstrations and sit-ins. Or, to give another example, she grants that saving the lives of the innocent warrants lying and deception but wonders what the right thing to do in less extreme situations is. Another source of moral uncertainty is the presence of dilemmas. It is not uncommon to become involved in situations in which discharging an autonomic obligation to A implies failing to discharge the same obligation (or an obligation of the same moral weight) to B or in situations in which she has to determine which unavoidable affront to someone's autonomy is the lesser evil. In cases like the above, there are no perfectly correct answers in the sense that whatever her choice, she will bring about (or allow to happen) a morally undesirable outcome. Finally, she realizes that sometimes the rightness of her decisions may be determined by future events of which she has no control. Yet, even if none of these complications adversely affects her moral deliberation, the very process of applying these general principles to particular cases presents its own difficulties. For instance, what exactly does her obligation not to discriminate against people on grounds of race or ethnicity imply? Should she just abstain from any sort of racist behavior or should she support the preferential treatment of disadvantaged minorities living in her country? Perhaps our moral subject will find proper or tenable answers to some of these vexing questions. However, at every step of her deliberation and despite her good intentions, the possibility of error looms large and much will turn on the nature of the situations she confronts. The moral image undoubtedly provides her with a general pattern of moral deliberation that comes down to general obligations but it cannot offer much help at the stage of their specification and application. It sets certain limits on her actions by making clear to her that no matter what others do, they deserve respect as autonomous beings,[3] but within these limits she has to make her own decisions.

The post-Kantian moral subject also considers the possibility of participating in real practical dialogues to find out whether there can be a *common agreement* concerning the specification and application of autonomic obligations to particular cases. However, once a dialogical procedure among real persons is initiated, she realizes that unbridgeable differences, which could not arise in a kingdom of common ends, come to the fore. First and foremost, the other participants may not share her autonomic obligations. Yet even when there is a shared normative background, there might be considerable disagreement concerning empirical facts and, when the stakes are high, it is not uncommon for the participants to show intransigence, syllogistic dishonesty, hypocrisy and bad faith. In addition, she is put off by the difficulty people have in accepting the consequences of the values they profess to endorse and she is worried by the fact that participants enter the dialogue with unequal argumentative powers. She tends to agree with Schopenhauer (1989, 728), who pointed out a long time ago that in a dispute that aims at finding truth, let alone moral truth, "the interest for truth…gives way entirely to the interest of vanity" and eventually man "fights not for truth but for his proposition". And finally she becomes convinced that actual moral dialogues are likely to lead to an impasse or to a compromise dictated by expediency[4] or self-interest. All these lead our subject to dismiss actual dialogical procedures as a criterion for the legitimization of particular moral rules or decisions based on autonomic obligations.[5] From this denial it does not follow that our subject shuns discussion or that she believes that she has nothing to gain from the views and arguments of others. She is not isolated from her social environment. Rather she considers herself responsible for her moral decisions and is willing to act contrary to the prevailing opinion. She is ready to justify her choices to others but she does not consider their consent as a necessary or sufficient requirement for moral action. Along with Kantian ethics our moral image is basically monological.

Returning now to Kantian ethics, we observe that what most worries Kant is our difficulty to overcome the emotions, instincts and inclinations which prevent us from complying with the moral law. Yet for him the commands of the moral law are clear and, roughly speaking, agents do not appear to be in doubt as to what they are supposed to do. Moreover, in the kingdom of ends in which we participate as rational beings, no disputes seem to arise as to whether a maxim could become a universal law or in respect to the practical meaning of the imperative to regard oneself and humanity as an end in itself. As far as perfect duties are concerned, their content is minutely specified in advance and becomes impervious to questioning. Only in regard to imperfect duties does Kant let slip an element of uncertainty by allowing the possibility of mistakes despite the agent's good intentions.

By following a more down-to-earth approach involving non-idealized agents, the post-Kantian moral image undermines most of the above Kantian certainties. As we have seen, the post-Kantian moral subject encounters significant setbacks and difficulties in putting into practice the autonomic obligations she endorses, and her predicament may not be due to her lack of motivation or to a weak will but to the recalcitrance and the ambiguity of the morally interesting situations she comes across. She also realizes that agreement on the particulars of morals cannot be easily achieved, once we have to deal with real people and not with idealized abstractions. These are dismal findings, but it is better to face them than to pretend that they do not exist. In addition, the principles established by the moral image outlined here stand on firmer ground, as every effort has been taken to avoid metaphysical considerations and untenable positions such as moral absolutism. After all, feasible autonomy appears to be more accessible, familiar and attractive to most of us than an a priori moral law of unknown origin, and there is considerable empirical evidence to support our ability to feel genuine sympathetic concern for our fellow humans.

Perhaps one might form the impression that our moral image offers inadequate moral guidance, as it does not go beyond positing certain prima facie general obligations. This, however, does not apply, since it is my belief that if a significant number of individuals and institutions start acting systematically and consistently according to these obligations, things will be improved for everyone, despite the inevitable conflicts, disappointments, failures and mishaps. The post-Kantian moral image calls on us to fight the major evils besetting our planet such as gratuitous and excessive violence, poverty and exploitation, lack of democratic self-governance, disease and illiteracy, and various forms of bigotry without having to secure everyone's prior consent about what ought to be done in each case. Obviously, it does not help us in deciding the morality of abortion, euthanasia or reproductive cloning. But, although it is not my wish to downplay the moral gravity of these issues, I reckon that from a global perspective the continuous disputes surrounding such issues do not bear heavily on the "moral deficit" of the world today.

4.2. Possible objections

I will now consider two general objections that could be raised against the post-Kantian moral image. First, someone might argue that the emphasis put on autonomy unduly restricts the scope of our obligations. It could be maintained that children and the mentally ill—to mention two broad categories of persons not counted among the autonomous—do not have a place in it, and, in addition, that it clings to speciesism as it is unlikely, as far as we can tell, for non-human animals to pursue approved life plans. Thus, the argument continues, we pave the way for treating all these subjects only as means to our ends. To begin with humans, the first thing to be said against this criticism is that autonomy is a matter of degree.[6] This means that people vary significantly in regard to the aspects of their lives over which they exercise autonomous control. From a certain age onwards, children can be regarded as having certain autonomously chosen, simple, short-term projects, such as those related to daily habits, play and entertainment, but children are unable for the most part to undertake complex, long-term projects, due to limited temporal horizon and lack of the required abilities and skills. They cannot start their own business but they can choose what game to play or what clothes to wear. It would be a gross underestimation of children to regard them as totally immature and to believe that they have to follow our instructions in everything. In addition, it should not escape our attention that children of every age are not just capable of autonomy but they are in the *process* of developing it. Thus, if the post-Kantian moral subject values autonomy, she has to intervene in children's lives in ways that would secure the conditions for the formation of autonomous personalities.[7] The autonomic obligations concern children as well, even if she may not apply them the same way she applies them to adults.

Along similar lines it could be held that mental illness does not by fiat deprive people of their autonomy by making them totally incompetent. Many patients with mental disorders retain various degrees of autonomy and most of them have considered and feasible plans of life and reasonably believe that their pursuit will contribute to their own good.[8] The fact that these projects may not appear to promote their interests, as we understand them, or to promote them in the most efficient way[9] does not prove their lack of autonomy. The important thing is that these plans and the relevant beliefs to be *their own* in the sense of not being caused by a specified medical condition determining their behavior. Thus, the mentally ill are not excluded from the scope of autonomic obligations and those institutionally responsible for them have the special duty to restore their impaired autonomy as far as possible and to help them gain control over significant aspects of their lives.

Of course, it cannot be denied that there are individuals who lack autonomy and their condition is irreversible. We can think of the comatose and of those suffering from severe mental retardation.[10] The sight of these people evokes our subject's sympathy and she is thus motivated to do something to alleviate their suffering and make their lives bearable. Most autonomic obligations do not apply in their case, but the sympathy she feels for them commits her to care about their well-being.

Proceeding now to the charge of speciesism, I would like to stress that the post-Kantian moral image fares better than rationalist and contractualist moral theories. As we have seen, the suffering of others motivates the post-Kantian moral subject, and, as there are common forms of suffering between human and non-human animals, there is nothing to prevent her from feeling sympathy for the latter. Moreover, she does not have to identify with the mental states of animals, whatever they are, to be motivated by their condition. Of course a sympathy-based animal ethics would have to deal successfully with the disgust we feel at the sight of certain harmless animals, which makes us indifferent to their suffering. Also it has to decide whether the painless killing of animals to satisfy our nutritional needs constitutes a violation of our obligations to them. These issues cannot be discussed here but the important thing to note is that the post-Kantian moral image does not rule out the expression of moral concern for animals.[11]

A second objection is that the post-Kantian moral image is parochial, as our subject relies on Western values that have little appeal to members of other cultures. This is a common criticism which cultural relativists address to all claims of moral universality and it deserves our attention. I have to say in advance that the suggested image is not to be met with enthusiasm by various people in various cultures, Western and non-Western alike. It is not easy for those who believe that there are no moral principles outside religion or those who divide people into faithful and unfaithful, "friends" and "enemies", white and colored and so forth to feel attracted to it. However, what I cannot accept is that the moral image is dismissed out of hand by anyone who just happens to participate in a different culture.

Sympathy, viewed either as an emotion or as a moral notion, appears to transcend cultural bounds. It has been maintained that empathy, which is sympathy's developmentally anterior stage, presupposes a common human physiology so that

> it seems reasonable to conclude that although empathy's prosocial motive property has only been studied in the United States, empathy must be considered a prime candidate for being a universal motive base for prosocial moral behavior when humans observe others in distress (Hoffman 2000, 274).

Also at the level of ideas we encounter various conceptions of sympathy in many cultures. To give an example, in the Buddhist and in the Hindu tradition there is a conception of sympathy (*ahimsa*) which covers every form of life and is based on the metaphysical assumption that there is no clear-cut ontological distinction between the self and other beings (Peetush, 2003). And it is important to note that some of the moral assertions deriving from conceptions of this kind are not necessarily unwelcome to Western philosophers.[12]

The charge of parochialism appears more convincing when it focuses on the notion of autonomy, since this appears to be a rather recent Western invention.[13] However, just because an ideal emerged at a certain point in the intellectual history of the West, we cannot infer that it is impossible to be disseminated and find supporters in other parts of the globe.[14] History bears witness to this. Popular ideals are not "trade marks" prohibiting unauthorized use and cultures are rarely so homogeneous and impenetrable as to prevent the reception of imported ideas effectively. As Steven Lukes (2003, 19-20) so poignantly observes:

> One should never forget that the simplifying perception of the internal coherence and distinctness of cultures from one another is in-

variably perpetrated by interested parties—by cultural entrepreneurs, by priests and elders, by populist and nationalist intellectuals and propagandists, and even by social anthropologists in search of unified and uncontaminated objects of study.

Along these lines one could discern two routes through which a sense of individual autonomy could begin to have an impact on societies in which rigid hierarchies or collectivist values prevail. The first is a "downward" route and it concerns the efforts of local elites to implement liberal and democratic reforms. I have already referred to the social dimension of autonomy and it is now an established fact that popular sovereignty and the rule of law offer individuals the opportunity to control significant aspects of their lives that were under someone else's control in autocracies.[15] Recall that the whole gamut of rights (civil, political and social) protects individuals from what they do not want to happen to them and provides them with certain all-purpose means to pursue their plans. Of course, an autonomy culture is not to be established overnight but it is not unreasonable to believe that the wave of democratization that started in the eighties will help many people all over the world to begin to perceive in practice the value of autonomy. Moreover, there is another "upward" route that appears more promising in countries in which there is economic growth but no democratic reforms. Those who prosper from a thriving market economy may obtain a sense of consumer autonomy. Undoubtedly, in many cases this is just an *illusion,* given the artificial character of many consumer needs, the inadequate information most people have and the manipulative character of advertising. Nevertheless, for persons whose autonomy has been deliberately kept at a minimum, for example most women in Third World countries, the novel possibility of carrying out certain consumer plans makes the value of autonomy attractive to them. If this is combined with a higher level of general literacy, it is possible for autonomy—envisaged, of course, not as a philosophical concept but as a way of life—to take hold among the younger strata of populations in the long run. For instance, if young girls successfully started to resist pre-arranged marriages, as has happened in the past in the West, this would be a small victory for autonomy.[16] The role of Western countries in the dissemination of autonomy is not negligible but this is not something that can be discussed here.

Coming now to autonomic obligations, it is evident that some of them, such as those which demand respect for human life, are not new but are well entrenched in almost every culture, while others depend, of course, on the acceptance of the general assumption that other people are equally autonomous persons. It should be noted, however, that the suggested moral image is flexible, since it recognizes that the specification of autonomic obligations may be underdetermined by culture-specific factors. These remarks only open the discussion, but what is for certain is that the cultural relativist will not win her case by default.

In concluding this account, one thing that has to be clarified is the post-Kantian character of the suggested moral image. From Kant it retains the demand to respect persons qua persons, a modified conception of autonomy, the rejection of happiness as the fundamental principle of morals, the universalizability of obligations and the requirement that agents themselves should be able to give their own justification for their maxims of action. However, it goes beyond Kant (a) by avoiding the four controversial Kantian assumptions outlined in the second chapter and (b) by regarding the emotion of sympathy as necessary for entering the moral realm.

As far as the image's plausibility is concerned, it should be by now clear that it manages to derive from the notion of autonomy normative conclusions that are familiar to most people living in Western cultures. The advantage is that these conclusions are now presented as forming a coherent set and this helps interested individuals in their reflective search for moral guidance.

4.3. Epilogue

Jonathan Glover (2001) brought to our attention the fact that at the dawn of the twenty-first century we cannot be as morally innocent as many philosophers were in the past. The tens of millions brutally and systematically killed during the last century do not allow this innocence, and the first years of the new century do not justify an optimistic outlook. This warning, as I understand it, when applied to ethical discourse calls for moderation, reserve, and respect for certain facts of human psychology. It also means that ethical discourse cannot be envisaged as a complex intellectual game cherished by only a few academic players. On the other hand, philosophical ethics cannot shrink from arguing about how things *should* be. And to convey the simile of Neurath's boat[17] to our topic, I could say that moral argumentation should necessarily rely on materials we find in our vessel, as we cannot reach any transcendent safe harbor. Nevertheless, there is no shortage of materials and we have to select the most appropriate combination for our predicament. Through this perspective I believe that a concise pattern of moral thought woven around a plausible and down-to-earth interpretation of the key-notions of autonomy and sympathy could have a chance, if adopted, to keep our vessel seaworthy, despite our unavoidable moral fallibility.

Notes

1. Of course it should not escape our attention that the experience of sympathy can be hindered by various factors such as fear, hate, despair, continuous exposure to human suffering or because the agent has been trained to suppress her emotions (as it often happens in military training). Moreover, it is possible for certain features of the situation the agent encounters to block the emergence of this emotion (Doris 2002, 28-34). Finally, there might be individuals who are totally incapable of feeling sympathy, such as certain psychopaths, but their number must be very limited. I assume that our moral subject does not belong to the last category and that there are no general factors permanently obstructing the display of her sympathetic concern for others.
2. In recent philosophical literature the idea of combining not sympathy but empathy with autonomy is discussed, as far as I can tell, in the works of Deigh (1995) and Slote (2004). Deigh claims in passing that children capable of empathy are able to see "the purposes that give extension and structure to the other's life...as worthwhile" and thus they "come to recognize others as autonomous agents and to participate imaginatively in their separate lives" (760). Slote, who goes into more detail, argues that "the ethics of empathic caring has (or can have) a distinctive way of understanding individual autonomy that is both attractive and plausible in its own right" (301). One crucial difference between my approach and Slote's is that in his work autonomy is kept subordinated to empathic caring (the analog of my sympathetic concern). In practice, this means that respect for autonomy depends entirely and without exception on the empathy we can feel for others, something that does not apply to my account. The autonomic obligations I discuss in this chapter are not limited to people for whom we feel sympathy. Sympathy helps only in recognizing autonomy as a universal value.
3. Cf. Hill's remark (1997, 65) that "from a moral point of view...it is generally worse to risk denying respect where it is due than to risk granting respect where it is not due".
4. To highlight the last point I offer the discussions that took place in the United Nations among state representatives and that ended in the *Declaration on the Elimination of All Forms of Intolerance and of Discrimination Based on Religion or Belief* proclaimed by the General Assembly in 1981. For the sake of reaching an agreement, participants decided to leave out normatively important clauses that had been included in previous official United Nations documents. Thus there was no reference to the right to change one's religion and the statement that atheism counts as "belief" was omitted. For those participants who believed that religious freedom is inconceivable without the above right or without legitimizing atheism was the final text not a compromise of their moral beliefs? What's more, Iran made it clear that it did recognize this agreement to

the extent that it was compatible with Islamic law! See *Yearbook of the United Nations* (1981, 879-83).

5. Presumably, she would reject the basic principle of Habermas's discourse ethics that "only those norms can claim to be valid that meet (or could meet) with the approval of all affected in their capacity *as participants in a practical discourse*" (Habermas 1990, 66).

6. It goes without saying that the sole purpose of the remarks that follow is to show that children and those suffering from mild mental disorders are not excluded by the post-Kantian moral image. How we should discharge our autonomic obligations to them is a different issue that lies beyond the confines of the current argument.

7. For the radical implications of taking children's autonomy seriously, see Lindley (1986, chap. 8).

8. See among others Lindley (1986, chap. 9) and Mittler (1991). For those of us who do not have experience with the mentally ill, Steinbeck's novel *Of Mice and Men* (1937) can prove illuminating. One of its main characters is Lenny, a simple-minded person with limited self-control who is dependent on his friend George. Nevertheless, this person has formed and tries to pursue specific and reasonable plans of life that give meaning and purpose to his miserable routine.

9. Cf. Silver's (2002, 465) claim that "competency, the right to run your own life, really should be based on nothing more than your capacity to run your own life, not your capacity to do it well".

10. The two cases are not normatively identical for we are able to treat the comatose as if they were autonomous, if they have given an advance directive about how they would like to be treated in case something similar happened to them.

11. Recently Ian Hacking (2001) suggested that animal rights theories run into significant philosophical difficulties and thus they should be abandoned in favor of a sympathy-based approach. One of his major claims is that we ought not to be moved only by animal suffering, but that "it is important to have a reasonable range of sympathies such that one can resonate to the state of the animal" (703). It is worth noting that although Kant condemns cruel treatment of animals, he believes that the relevant duties are not duties to animals but duties to ourselves (MM, VI: 443, 564). For him maltreatment to animals predisposes us badly in respect to our moral stance to our fellow humans.

12. Cf. Walsh-Frank's (1996) article in which she claims that the conception of compassion adopted by the Buddhist school *Mahayana* should be preferred to its Western counterpart put forward by Lawrence Blum. Works of this kind indicate that certain Western and non-Western conceptions of sympathy are not incommensurable in principle.

13. Nevertheless, it has been suggested (Chan 2002) that in Confucianism there is to be found a conception of moral autonomy in the sense of voluntary endorsement of a reflective approach to moral life.

14. See Franck (1997).

15. John Stuart Mill in his *Considerations of representative government* (1861) was one of the first philosophers who argued that the democracy of the moderns is the best form of government for it makes people self-protecting, self-dependent and responsible, and it gives them the opportunity to exercise and improve their intellectual faculties.

16. Amarthya Sen (1999) has documented how literacy helps Indian women in exercising better control over family planning.

17. "We are like sailors who have to rebuild their ship on the open sea, without ever being able to dismantle it in dry-dock and reconstruct it from the best components" (Neurath 1983, 92).

Bibliography

Allison, Henry E. 1990. *Kant's theory of freedom*. Cambridge: Cambridge University Press.
Baron, Marcia W. 1995. *Kantian ethics almost without apology*. Ithaca and London: Cornell University Press.
———. 1997. Kantian ethics. In Marcia W. Baron, Philip Pettit, and Michael Slote *Three methods of ethics*. Oxford: Blackwell.
Batson, Daniel C. 1991. *The altruism question: Toward a social-psychological answer*. Hillsdale: Lawrence Erlbaum Associates.
Batson, Daniel C., and Moran, Tecia. 1999. Empathy-induced altruism in a prisoner's dilemma. *European Journal of Social Psychology* 29: 909-24.
Ben-Ze'ev, Aaron. 2000. *The subtlety of emotions*. Cambridge, Mass.: The MIT Press.
Bittner, Rüdiger. 1989. *What reason demands*. Trans. Theodore Talbot. Cambridge: Cambridge University Press.
Blum, Lawrence. 1980. Compassion. In *Explaining emotions*. Ed. Amélie Oksenberg Rorty. Berkeley: University of California Press.
Cassirer, Ernst. 1981. *Kant's life and thought*. Trans. James Haden. New Haven and London: Yale University Press.
Chan, Joseph. 2002. Moral autonomy, civil liberties and Confucianism. *Philosophy East and West* 52: 281-310.
Chismar, Douglas. 1988. Empathy and sympathy: The important difference. *The Journal of Value Inquiry* 22: 257-66.
Cottingham, John. 1998. *Philosophy and the good life: Reason and the passions in Greek, Cartesian and psychoanalytic ethics*. Cambridge: Cambridge University Press.
Crisp, Roger. 2003. Equality, priority and compassion. *Ethics* 113: 745-63.
Crittenden, Jack. 1993. The social nature of autonomy. *The Review of Politics* 55: 35-65.

Damasio, Antonio R. 1994. *Descartes' error: Emotion, reason, and the human brain*. New York: Avon Books.
Darwall, Stephen. 1998. Empathy, sympathy, care. *Philosophical Studies* 89: 261-82.
De Sousa, Ronald. 1990. *The rationality of emotion*. Cambridge, Mass.: The MIT Press.
Deigh, John. 1995. Empathy and universalizability. *Ethics* 105: 743-63.
Descartes, René. 1650/1985. *The passions of the soul*. In *The philosophical writings of Descartes*. Trans. John Cottingham, Robert Stoothoff, and Dugald Murdoch. Vol. 1. Cambridge: Cambridge University Press.
Doris, John M. 2002. *Lack of character: Personality and moral behavior*. Cambridge: Cambridge University Press.
Dworkin, Gerald. 1988. *The theory and practice of autonomy*. Cambridge: Cambridge University Press.
Elster, Jon. 1996. Rationality and the emotions. *The Economic Journal* 106: 1386-97.
Feinberg, Joel. 1986. *Harm to self*. The moral limits of the criminal law. Vol. III. New York: Oxford University Press.
Foot, Philippa. 1978. *Virtues and vices and other essays in moral philosophy*. Oxford: Blackwell.
Franck, Thomas M. 1997. Is personal freedom a western value? *The American Journal of International Law* 91: 593-627.
Frankfurt, Harry G. 1971. Freedom of the will and the concept of a person. *The Journal of Philosophy* 68: 5-20.
Galston, William A. 1993. What is living and what is dead in Kant's practical philosophy? In *Kant and political philosophy: The contemporary legacy*. Ed. Ronald Beiner and William James Booth. New Haven and London: Yale University Press.
Gill, Frances E. 2000. Moral reason and sympathy. *Southwest Philosophy Review* 16: 153-64.
Glover, Jonathan. 2001. *Humanity: A moral history of the twentieth century*. New Haven and London: Yale University Press.
Goldie, Peter. 2000. *The emotions: A philosophical exploration*. Oxford: Clarendon Press.
Goldman, Alvin I. 1993. *Philosophical applications of cognitive science*. Boulder: Westview Press.
Goleman, Daniel. 1997. *Emotional intelligence: Why it can matter more than IQ*. New York: Bantam Books.
Guyer, Paul, ed. 1998. *Kant's Groundwork of the metaphysics of morals: Critical essays*. Lanham: Rowman and Littlefield.

Habermas, Jürgen. 1990. *Moral consciousness and communicative action.* Trans. Christian Lenhardt and Shierry Weber Nicholsen. Intr. Thomas McCarthy. Cambridge: Polity Press.

———. 1993. *Justification and application: Remarks on discourse ethics.* Trans. Ciaran P. Cronin. Cambridge: Polity Press.

Hacking, Ian. 2001. On sympathy: With other creatures. *Tijdschrift voor Filosofie* 63: 685-717.

Hare, R. M. 1997. *Sorting out ethics.* Oxford: Clarendon Press.

Haritos-Fatouros, Mika. 2002. *The psychological origins of institutionalized torture.* London: Routledge.

Haworth, Lawrence. 1986. *Autonomy: An essay in philosophical psychology and ethics.* New Haven and London: Yale University Press.

Hegel, G. W. F. 1802-1803/1975. *Natural law.* Trans. T. M. Knox. Intr. H. B. Acton. Philadelphia: University of Pennsylvania Press.

Henrich, Dieter. 1992. *Aesthetic judgment and the moral image of the world: Studies in Kant.* Stanford: Stanford University Press.

Herman, Barbara. 1993. *The practice of moral judgment.* Cambridge, Mass.: Harvard University Press.

———. 1998. Training to autonomy: Kant and the question of moral education. In *Philosophers on education: New historical perspectives.* Ed. A. Oksenberg Rorty. London: Routledge.

Hill, Thomas E. Jr. 1992. *Dignity and practical reason in Kant's moral philosophy.* Ithaca and London: Cornell University Press.

———. 1997. Respect for humanity. In *The Tanner lectures on human values* . Ed. Grethe B. Peterson. Vol. 18. Salt Lake City: University of Utah Press.

———. 1999. Happiness and human flourishing in Kant's ethics. *Social Philosophy and Policy* 16: 143-75.

Höffe, Otfried. 1994. *Immanuel Kant.* Trans. Marshall Farrier. New York: State University of New York Press.

———, hrsg. 2002. *Kant, Immanuel: Kritik der praktischen Vernuft.* Berlin: Akademie Verlag.

Hoffman, Martin L. 2000. *Empathy and moral development: Implications for caring and justice.* Cambridge: Cambridge University Press.

Hume, David. 1739-1740/2000. *A treatise of human nature.* Eds. David Fate Norton and Mary J. Norton. Oxford: Oxford University Press.

Johnston, David. 1994. *The idea of liberal theory: A critique and reconstruction.* Princeton: Princeton University Press.

Korsgaard, Christine M. 1996. *Creating the kingdom of ends*. Cambridge: Cambridge University Press.
Lindley, Richard. 1986. *Autonomy*. Houndmills: Macmillan.
Lukes, Steven. 2003. *Liberals and cannibals: The implications of diversity*. London: Verso.
Malikiosi-Loizos, Maria. 2003. A critical look at empathy (in Greek). *Psychology* 10: 295-309.
Mele, Alfred R. 2001. *Autonomous agents: From self-control to autonomy*. Oxford: Oxford University Press.
Mercer, Philip. 1972. *Sympathy and ethics: A study of the relationship between sympathy and morality with special reference to Hume's Treatise*. Oxford: Clarendon Press.
Milgram, Stanley. 1974. *Obedience to authority: Experimental views*. New York: Harper and Row.
Mill, John Stuart. 1861/1998. *Utilitarianism*. Ed. Roger Crisp. Oxford: Oxford University Press.
Mittler, Peter. 1991. Competence and consent in people with mental handicap. In *Protecting the vulnerable: Autonomy and consent in health care*. Eds. Margaret Brazier and Mary Lobjoit. London and New York: Routledge.
Monroe, Kristen Renwick. 1996. *The heart of altruism: Perceptions of a common humanity*. Princeton: Princeton University Press.
Nagel, Thomas. 1979. *Mortal questions*. Cambridge: Cambridge University Press.
Neurath, Otto. 1983. *Philosophical papers 1913-1946*. Ed. Robert S. Cohen and Marie Neurath. Dordrecht: Reidel.
Nozick, Robert. 1974. *Anarchy, state, and utopia*. Oxford: Blackwell.
Nussbaum, Martha C. 2001. *Upheavals of thought: The intelligence of emotions*. Cambridge: Cambridge University Press.
Oakley, Justin. 1993. *Morality and the emotions*. London and New York: Routledge.
O' Neill, Onora. 1989. *Constructions of reason: Explorations in Kant's practical philosophy*. Cambridge: Cambridge University Press.
―――. 1997. Kant on reason and religion. In *The Tanner lectures on human values*. Ed. Grethe B. Peterson. Vol. 18. Salt Lake City: University of Utah Press
―――. 2002. *Autonomy and trust in bioethics*. Cambridge: Cambridge University Press.
Peetush, Ashwani Kumar. 2003. Cultural diversity, non-Western communities, and human rights. *The Philosophical Forum* 34: 1-19.

Peonidis, Filimon. 1994. *Lying and morality* (in Greek). Thessaloniki: Vanias.
———. 2005. Autonomy and sympathy: Towards a post-Kantian moral humanism. *Journal of Philosophical Research* 30 (forthcoming).
Putnam, Hilary. 1987. *The many faces of realism*. La Salle: Open Court.
Rachels, James. 1997. *Can ethics provide the answers? And other essays in moral philosophy*. Lanham: Rowman and Littlefield.
Rawls, John. 1973. *A theory of justice*. Oxford: Oxford University Press.
Raz, Joseph. 1986. *The morality of freedom*. Oxford: Clarendon Press.
Reath, Andrews. 1997. Legislating for a realm of ends: The social dimension of autonomy. In *Reclaiming the history of ethics: Essays for John Rawls*. Eds. Andrews Reath, Barbara Herman, and Christine M. Korsgaard. Cambridge: Cambridge University Press.
———. 1998. Autonomy, ethical. In *Routledge encyclopaedia of philosophy*. Ed. Edward Craig. London and New York: Routledge.
Scheler, Max. 1912/1970. *The nature of sympathy*. Trans. Peter Heath. Intr. W. Stark. London: Routledge.
Schneewind, Jerome B. 1998. *The invention of autonomy*. New York: Cambridge University Press.
Schopenhauer, Arthur. 1841/1998. *On the basis of morality*. Trans. E. F. J. Payne. Intr. David E. Cartwright. Indianapolis: Hackett.
———. 1989. Eristic dialectic. In *Manuscript remains in four volumes*. Ed. Arthur Hübscher. Trans. E. F. J. Payne. Vol. 3. Berlin manuscripts (1818-1830). Oxford: Berg.
Sen, Amarthya. 1996. Fertility and coercion. *University of Chicago Law Review* 63: 1035-61.
Sherman, Nancy. 1997. *Making a necessity of virtue: Aristotle and Kant on virtue*. Cambridge: Cambridge University Press.
Silver, Mitchell. 2002. Reflections on determining competency. *Bioethics* 16: 455-68.
Slote, Michael. 2003. Sentimentalist virtue and moral judgement: Outline of a project. *Metaphilosophy* 34: 131-43.
———. 2004. Autonomy and empathy. *Social Philosophy and Policy* 21: 293-309.
Smith, Adam. 1759/1984. *The theory of moral sentiments*. Eds. D. D. Raphael and A. L. Macfie. Indianapolis: Liberty Fund.

Sober, Elliot, and Wilson, David Sloan. 1999. *Unto others: The evolution and psychology of unselfish behaviour.* Cambridge, Mass.: Harvard University Press.
Sullivan, Roger J. 1989. *Immanuel Kant's moral theory.* Cambridge: Cambridge University Press.
Taylor, Craig. 2002. *Sympathy: A philosophical analysis.* Houndmills: Palgrave-Macmillan.
Timmons, Mark, ed. 2002. *Kant's Metaphysics of morals: Interpretative essays.* Oxford: Clarendon Press.
Tudor, Steven. 2001. *Compassion and remorse: Acknowledging the suffering other.* Leuven: Peeters.
Vetlesen, Arne Johan. 1994. *Perception, empathy, and judgment: An inquiry into the preconditions of moral performance.* University Park: The Pennsylvania State University Press.
Walsh-Frank, Patricia. 1996. Compassion: An East-West comparison. *Asian Philosophy* 6: 5-16.
Williams, Bernard. 1985. *Ethics and the limits of philosophy.* London: Fontana Press.
Wispè, Lauren. 1991. *The psychology of sympathy.* New York: Plenum Press.
Wood, Allen W. 1999. *Kant's ethical thought.* Cambridge: Cambridge University Press.
Young, Robert. 1986. *Personal autonomy: Beyond negative and positive liberty.* London and Sydney: Croom Helm.

Index

Allison, H. E., 24-25
autonomic obligations, 60-65
autonomy, 12, 14, 29-30, 34-38, 40-41, 60-73
aversive arousal reduction, 52

Baron, M., 23, 24, 55
Batson, D. C., 52-53, 57
Ben-Ze'ev, A., 43, 47, 48, 55, 56
Bittner, R., 30
Blum, L., 49, 50, 56, 72
Buddhism, 67, 72
Butler, J., 51

Cassirer, E., 23
categorical imperative, 5-17, 23, 27, 28, 32
Chan, J., 72
children, 65
Chismar, D., 55
compassion, see sympathy
Confucianism, 72
Cottingham, J., 55
Crisp, R., 56
Crittenden, J., 40
cultural relativism, 66

Damasio, A. R., 44
Darwall, S., 56
De Sousa, R., 44

deception, 11
Deigh, J. 71
Descartes, R., 43, 55
dignity, 12
discourse ethics, 27, 72
discrimination, 61, 62
Doris, J. M., 71
doxastic self-control, 40
duty, 4, 20-22, 39, 61-62
Dworkin, R., 40

Elster, J., 44, 47
emotional intelligence, 44
emotions, 43-44
empathy, 48-49, 55, 67
empathy-altruism hypothesis, 52
evolutionary biology, 56
exploitation, 11, 24

feelings, 47
Feinberg, J., 24
Foot, P., 32
Franck, T. M., 73
Frankfurt, H., 40
freedom, 13-17, 25

Galston, W. A., 27
Gill, F. E., 50, 56
Glover, J., 54, 69
God, 18-20

Goldie, P., 49, 56
Goldman, A., 56
Goleman, D., 44
good will, 3-4
Guyer, P., 23

Habermas, J., 27, 72
Hacking, I., 72
happiness, 18-20, 69
hard paternalism, 11
Hare, R. M., 27
Haritos-Fatouros, M., 41
Haworth, L., 36, 40
Hegel, G. W. F., 39
Heine, H., 25
Henrich, D., 40
Herman, B., 23, 25
heterogeneity of values, 28
highest good, 18
Hill, T. E., 23, 25, 39, 71
Hinduism, 67
Hobbes, T., 51
Höffe, O., 23
Hoffman, M. L., 51-52, 67
Hume, D., 31, 47, 55
hypothetical imperative, 6, 32

Johnston, D., 39
justice as fairness, 27

Kant, I., 1-25, 27-32, 39, 40, 43-47, 49, 51, 55, 64, 69, 72
kingdom of ends, 12, 29, 39, 63
Korsgaard, C. M., 23, 31

Leibniz, G. W., 60
liberty, 40
Lindley, R., 72
Lukes, S., 67-68
lying, 11, 25, 62

Malikiosi-Loizos, M., 48
manipulation, 36-37, 68
maxim, 4-13, 23, 24
Mele, A. R., 40
mental illness, 48, 66
Mercer, P., 50, 56
Milgram, S., 41
Mill, J. S., 23, 43, 56, 73
Mittler, P., 72
Monroe, K. R., 56
moral absolutism, 28, 39, 64
moral deficit, 65
moral dialogue, 63
moral dilemmas, 62
moral image (defined), 32-33, 40
moral innocence, 69
moral law, 4, 13, 16-17, 24, 30, 64
moral luck, 6
moral saint, 60
Moran, T., 57

Nagel, T., 28
nature, 24
Nazism, 54
Neurath's boat, 69, 73
Nozick, R., 27
Nussbaum, M., 43, 49, 54, 56, 57

Oakley, J., 54, 56
O' Neill, O., 23, 25, 39

parochialism, 66-69
Peetush, A. K., 67
Peonidis, F., 25, 40
pity, 55
Plato, 43
post-Kantian moral subject (defined), 33

practical reason, 5, 30-32, 40
preferential treatment, 62
prisoner's dilemma, 57
Putnam, H., 40

Rachels, J., 39
racism, 54, 63
Rawls, J., 27
Raz, J., 40
Reath, A., 36, 40
remorse, 55
respect, 1, 63, 69
rights, 27, 61, 68
Rousseau, J. J., 47

Scheler, M., 47, 56
Schneewind, J. B., 23
Schopenhauer, A., 47, 50, 63
Sen, A., 73
Sherman, N., 55
Silver, M., 72
Slote, M., 56, 71
Smith, A., 47, 48
Sober, E., 56
speciesism, 66
Steinbeck, J., 72
Sullivan, R. G., 17, 23
sympathy, 45-57, 59-60, 64, 66, 67, 69, 71, 72

Taylor, C., 47, 48
theoretical reason, 40
Timmons, M., 23
tolerance, 61, 62
Tudor, S., 55, 56

United Nations, 71-72
universalizability, 1, 69
utilitarianism, 27, 28

Vetlesen, A. J., 56

virtue, 20, 44
volition, 18, 40

Walsh-Frank, P., 72
Weir, P., 41
Williams, B., 40
Wilson, D. S., 56
Wispè, L., 56
Wood, A. W., 12, 23

Young, R., 36

About the author

Filimon Peonidis is an assistant professor of moral and political philosophy at the Aristotle University of Thessaloniki, his alma mater. He holds an M. Sc. from the London School of Economics and Political Science and a doctorate from the University of Crete. His primary academic interests are in moral philosophy with an emphasis on Mill, Kant and applied ethics, and in political philosophy with an emphasis on the history and theory of liberalism, and the philosophical foundations of free expression. His work in Greek includes a book on the morality of lying, an annotated translation of Mill's *Utilitarianism*, an edition of Constant's political writings and several articles on moral and political philosophy. His work in English includes the collective volume (co-edited with N. Avgelis) *Aristotle on language, logic and science* and articles published in journals such as the *Journal of Value Inquiry, Law and Philosophy, History of Political Thought*, the *Journal of Social Philosophy* and the *Journal of Philosophical Research*.

www.ingramcontent.com/pod-product-compliance
Lightning Source LLC
Chambersburg PA
CBHW022016300426
44117CB00005B/223